3-14-60

I N D I A

toward an understanding

INDIA

toward an understanding

....

A *de novo* inquiry into the mind of India
In search of an answer to the question:
"Will India go Communist?"

....

GEORGE K. CHACKO

BOOKMAN ASSOCIATES
NEW YORK

Dedicated To
My Beloved Mother Thankamma
Whose affectionate understanding of me
Abides, transcending time and space

1112193

PREFACE

Suddenly, Tibet is in the news.

The theocracy at the top of the world is aflame in its struggle for survival as a free nation. Whether or not Tibet will succeed is for history to show. However, the heroic stand made by millions of Tibetans in defense of their fundamental rights is an affirmation of the spirit of mankind itself. It is the universality of their, as well as all of Asia's, present struggle that brings this remote area of the Himalayas close to the hearts and minds of freedom-loving people everywhere, and which has created the current focus of interest on events in the Middle East and Asia.

The most immediate consequences of Tibet's rebellion against tyranny are of greatest concern to her neighbor, India. The hurried flight to India of the Dalai Lama, god-king of the Tibetans, symbolizes the sanctuary of freedom which India represents to all Asia.

India's call to greatness, made by Tibet in her hour of distress to the largest free nation of Asia, is a challenge to India's inner resources. How India answers that call will be determined by the reactions of each and every Indian to a new way of life—political independence. The firmly rooted traditions of an ancient Eastern civilization must be modified to fit the aspirations of a newly independent India strongly influenced by Western commercial success and the resultant high standards of living.

However, the need for modification of these traditions has also attracted another powerful and militant ideology—international communism. For millions of semi-literate Indians the sudden disruption of a centuries-old way of life means confusion and personal chaos. At such a time the earliest apparent cure for the present ill tends to appear as the most attractive, and communism has always appeared to the naïve as the possessor of a universal panacea.

The experience of China, just across the Himalayas from India, is a warning to all of the danger of treating this threat lightly, for even now Indian followers of communism are engaged in efforts to overrun India by systematically destroying the ancient social fabric of the land just as was done in China.

Whether the outcome for India will be democracy or communism depends on the state of her inner stability. Thus, this volume presents an examination of the facets which make up this stability: religion, economics, politics, social institutions, and the state of the Indian mind itself. This, in turn, will answer, or aid in answering, a question of grave import for the free world: "Will India go Communist?"

CONTENTS

LIST OF TABLES

PART I

The Setting

PORTENTS AND PROMISES

HE HAD BEEN A COMMUNIST. Almost one year after relinquishing party membership he was still not accepted by the society of his origin. He was born and brought up as a member of one of the most ancient churches of Christendom. Tradition traced the founding of the church back to the year 52 A.D. Intellectually, he hailed from an elite: he was one of the very few who had received a university education. However, his former red association had left him very much alone with respect to acceptance by both the church constituent and the university element of his society.

A few years ago, when he went to join the Communist Party, they asked him, "Why do you want to be a Communist?" He replied, "Because I am a Christian."

Today he was explaining to the audience, comprised of members of his society of origin, the circumstances under which he joined the Party. He narrated this story:

The dog went in search of a master. It went to the horse, which could move so fast and majestically. The master was proud to show the dog around the vast territory over which he could move and the dog was happy. One day the dog happened to wander outside the territory, and the horse snapped down to stop him. There was a tiger living around that area!

13

The dog wanted a master; and so he could not be satisfied with the horse who would be deterred by another animal. The next day, the dog went to locate the new master. Dark and handsome, the tiger seemed powerful. However, one day, while roaming in the forest, the dog felt like serenading. The tiger immediately hushed him: "Sh—It's the lion!"

Lion? The dog wanted to meet someone who could hush the powerful tiger into silent watchfulness. The lion was impressive in his narrative of his kingship over the entire forest. At long last, thought the dog, somebody could really be a master.

This state of happy servantship did not last long. When the dog felt the urge to express himself in praise of the king of the forest, the sound of the hunter was heard by the lion. Silencing his devoted servant, the lion explained that a species called man was inconveniently around. The dog went to offer his allegiance to the lion-hunting man. The man showed the dog the outer porch which was to be his bedroom. There was a rustle around midnight. The dog's immediate reaction was to sound the alarm, which he did. In the past, all the former masters had lost no time in curbing any endeavor for such expression. But his latest master, the man, did nothing of the kind. Instead, he urged the dog to go ahead in hot pursuit. The dog had finally found his true master; from then on, he could express himself without fear or hindrance.

To the narrator, the Communist Party was the only one which gave the green signal to his own urge to express his social concern. The church and the churchman had proved themselves to be like the poor masters of the dog: they always sought to hush any efforts to sound the alarm.

This narrator hailed from a State in India which leads the nation in literacy. While the literacy rate for India as a whole is less than 20 per cent, the former State of Travancore, the narrator's birthplace, is over 85 per cent literate. This State also has the highest percentage of Christians, with nearly a third of the population tracing the founding of their church back to the first century A.D. Are literacy and Christianity the stuff of Communism?

Or, is it the low standards of living that breed communists? The thesis of this volume is that it is neither. This thesis is built around a search for the answer to the perennial question: "Will India go Communist?"

However, he is a bold prophet indeed who can answer this question affirmatively. India, awoken from the solemn traditions as old as the hills themselves, now finds herself in the center of the keenest ideological conflict of the twentieth century. This conflict presents so turbulent a prospect that a definite answer as to the outcome is at best a matter of conjecture. Therefore, the attempt here is not so much to answer the question as it is to examine closely certain subtler aspects of the Indian mind relevant to the final determination of this question. This probing will disclose some portents, and maybe some promises too.

If India appears to be oddly unruffled by the Communist threat, or seems relatively passive in her relations to Communism when compared to other countries, it is not all Stoicism. Beneath the unruffled exterior will be disclosed a poise of mind arising out of a different sense of time and of history. The outward appearance of susceptibility to new ideas sometimes obscures a certain resilience of view cherished inwardly. The apparently meaningless ritual of the peasant farmers emerges as a way of life; a way of worship.

But how far is the road of the educated but disillusioned person who turns Communist from this silent citadel against Communism? Is it not wishful thinking to attribute active concern over his freedom to the poor Indian peasant? How about the Grand Inquisitor?

Didst Thou forget that man prefers peace, and even death, to freedom of choice in the knowledge of good and evil? . . .

Thou didst promise them the bread of Heaven, but, I repeat
again, can it compare with earthly bread in the eyes of the
weak, ever sinful and ignoble race of man? [1]

It may be unfashionable to say that peace hath her victories.
India's answer to the threat of communism courts the disadvantage of trying to conquer raging violence with the soft dews
of non-violence. Sentimental? Cowardly? The answer must rest
on a careful examination of the Indian mind, and the subsequent evaluation of the ethos revealed.

Here then are both the portents and promises. There are
the portents of the disillusionment of the educated at the
quaint activity in matters of social concern; the ambivalence
of the free about their freedom; the misunderstanding which
is the price to be paid for the uniqueness of this national
experiment with truth.

Pitted against these portents are the promises to be found
in the ethos of India with its resilience of inward view; the
outspoken avowal of non-violent methods, and, as a consequence, the accepted disadvantage of having to fight violence
with non-violence; the sense of time and of history as the
context in which the eternal experiment of maintaining the
integrity of means which defy sacrifice to expediency or pro-
grammed activity is carried out.

When these portents and promises are weighed, which will
be found wanting in the balance—communism or democracy?

CHAPTER TWO

CONTEXT AND CONTENT

Resumé of the political context of international events and relations—differing economic orderings—differing political views—historic outlook and idealistic nature of the Indian mind—economic, political and religious intonations of Communism and India.

AN OUTLINE OF THE HISTORY of human thought relevant to the present state of affairs in international relations is essential to any understanding of the content of current exchanges in thought, word and deed.

"Poverty anywhere is a threat to prosperity everywhere" has been recognized as a prudent maxim for a good many years. But the unprecedented advance in technical progress that has shrunk the world beyond recognition by reducing time and space as factors of distance, has brought sub-human levels of subsistence closer to rolling luxury of life than ever before. For instance, the continent that was once called the Dark Continent of Africa, to signify the mystery shrouding it, is no longer dark: civilization has stepped into, and information has come out of that segment of the globe. The "holy cow" probably persists as the symbol representing India, but today fewer Americans ask for your feathers when you say that you are an Indian. The cataclysmic changes that rock the face of the earth have managed to permeate through thick walls of ignorance. While it is still easier to break an atom than a prejudice, the forces hammering on prejudicial ignorance are assuming ever increasing proportions. As a cumulative result of these operative influences, people know more about what is happening in the other parts of the world. And more than that, they realize that they can ill-afford to claim any exemption from the sweeping currents of international events.

This recognition of interdependence has taken active form in politics as well as in economics. Pière Dubè, in the fourteenth century, was one of the pioneers in foreshadowing international efforts at peace, for he realized that peace cannot be achieved piecemeal. The "Holy Alliance" was one of the early instances of corporate effort transcending national boundaries. The principle of "Balance of Power", once extremely popular in Europe, was again an acknowledgment, though negatively, of the need for international efforts for security. The First World War brought home to a strife-torn world in no uncertain terms, the need for restraint on the frightening Frankenstein of global warfare. Woodrow Wilson caused the word "Peace" to be engraved thrice on the walls of the League of Nations building. And, in another twenty-five years, the potentialities of the powers of destruction were shown even more clearly: peace was peeping out through atomic piles. The post-Second World War years have witnessed the regional recognition of the need for defensive alliances. The permutations and combinations of the alphabet which are used to christen these organizations— from NATO to SHAPE—bespeak the almost desperate need of man to avoid being hoist with his own petard. The transition from hot to cold war seems to have been a jump out of the fire into the frying pan.

While the recognition of international interdependence was being made in terms of defensive alliances by some nations, other nations were evolving a somewhat different outlook on the events in their world. When the world ate of the fruit of the tree of global war, nations first knew that they were naked, exposed to insecurity; this sent some of them into protective pacts of mutual security. Secondly, the world knew that many nations could not decide for themselves as to how they were going to be secure. After bearing the brunt of global bonfires with their own sinews, they felt that they should be able to decide matters for themselves. Defense, offense or neutrality and self-development was their own affair.

Thus the people under the shadow of political domination groped to see light, the light of freedom. Political emancipation was fought for under the banner of nationalism. It was the great affirmation of the primeval urge to live and not merely to survive. Once afoot, the forces gathered momentum until the impact overshadowed the horizon, particularly of the Asian and African continents. The sky is by no means clear today: the thunders of independence and the lightning flashes of its affirmation still reverberate throughout the world.

Old order does not yield place to new without a struggle: bitter, in many instances, bloody in a few, and blessed, shall we say, in a very, very few.

The differences in background, as well as procedure, make distinctive regional variations in the setting of the present international situation. Aspirations, abilities, and achievements are of the widest variety, and this necessitates planning of a diverse range in order to make effective development possible. The time was, for instance, when the promotion from colonial status to dominionhood was the cherished consummation of the political life of an Afro-Asian country. But the quickening of the pace of time occasioned the outgrowth from this primer of political training, and much more than a mere morsel of self-government was found indispensable to appease the nascent hunger of the *enfant terrible* of backward areas.

Changes in the needs in the economic domain are more subtle and appear to take much longer to make an impression on the prejudices of the people than do those of a political nature. The institution of a new economic order is almost sacrilegious when compared to the more established systems. Conformity to one or another of set patterns is implicitly taken for granted, and any kind of variation is frowned upon as heresy. But the fact is that the choice is not as much between white and black as between grey and grey.

That the choice, therefore, is not between capitalism and communism, but between varying degrees of both, is probably more clearly recognized than before. The intervention of the state with the initiative of the individual is no longer clearly demarcated. Varying degrees of state intervention are found to be necessary in order to maintain the freedom of enterprise. The mounting volume of anti-monopoly legislation in the United States is an instance in point. More interesting than the legislation is the legal interpretation of the laws themselves. The courts have a hard time interpreting what constitutes a monopolizing tendency. Where freedom ends and authoritarianism begins is almost a razor's edge, defying definition, owing to the dynamics of life. Social situations change, and so do the means of regulating them. Even within the course of a few years, the ordinary business of life alters its form so radically that the business community can always feel that it is more sinned against than sinner in exploiting the freedom of enterprise.

In the last analysis, it is by this difficulty—the final impossibility of preventing evasion—that . . . almost all systems of economic regulation since the dawn of history are defeated. Capitalist enterprise is the child of evasion; and on the long road from ancient smuggler to modern industrialist, the entrepreneur has learned more tricks than are easily reckoned with. [1]

It may be realistic to consider that the evasion of legislative restrictions is an attempt to counteract what the businessman feels to be an inroad upon his own prerogatives. And if the legislature in turn feels that the laws are defeated in their purpose, it would not be surprising if they vote stronger measures to combat defiance and deviance. The possibility of a chain reaction—stern laws; defiance of them; creation of sterner laws—is not entirely academic. If the chain is sufficiently long, it can certainly stifle the very initiative it is intended to protect. And when such a stifling occurs, it may be asked: Is this state-control or private enterprise?

It would seem that the degree of state control is not an adequate measure of freedom of enterprise. The direction, rather than the degree, seems to be the criterion. If it is the direction which is the indicator, by its very nature, it has to be related to the particular context. One may well ask: How tall is tall?

In this context of economic ordering, which does not permit the drawing of any sharp lines, the insistence on establishing similar patterns of economy over the rest of the world sharply displays its incongruity. The more obvious seems to be the more obscured. And the fact that other economic systems have not evolved along the same line as that of the United States economy appears to have been awfully obscure. An implied insistence that there is no salvation in any other system has tended to lend an unfortunate coloring to American economic aid. It has led to certain frustration on the part of the donor that the underdeveloped economies are not molded exactly in her image; and it has occasioned considerable ire to the recipient that she should have to conform to someone else's ideas. The decision that he who is not for us is against us, is perhaps sweepingly applied sometimes, almost to mean that he who does not shout aye for all which one says or thinks or does, is against one. One of the results of this is a broken image of America abroad, and dissatisfaction in America with progress abroad. The tinge of disappointment over the results in the economic sphere reflects estrangement arising out of very good hopes.

I am concerned at the sight of the two tremendous colossi, he declared. "The Soviet Union on the one hand is not just regarded as a big power but also as an ideological force bent on making other peoples see things its way."

The United States must of course be seen from another,

different basis, Mr. Nehru declared. "It certainly has no desire to expand its territory but like all big powers they have
the missionary spirit. They expect others to follow their will.
If they do not, they (the United States) feel hurt and think
something is wrong with the other man's thinking." [2]

Like every good thing, very good hopes have the property
of extremities in intensity. The hopes which are very good,
when frustrated, turn to desperation. Fratricidal animosities,
it might be mentioned, are the worst kind of estrangement; so
also, the very good hopes, when not fulfilled, give rise to a
very sharp critical mood. If the promise of an infant republic
to blossom into a delightful partner in the democratic way of
life appears to be a long time in coming, less patient minds
would tend to grab any easy and simple explanation. Differing
views on international situations will be directly traced to dissimilar economic placings. India's failure to vote against Russia
is explained in terms of the Communist lure for a poor country.

> What India is trying to say to the World is a constant chal-
> lenge to our powers of interpretation and can be repeated
> to both Moscow and Washington. It is the essence of our
> creed and fundamental to an understanding of our way of life
> as well as our political stand. You know what I think—the end
> in itself is not important—unless the means we follow to
> achieve the end are right. The countries of the Western
> World will do well to try to understand this. It is what you
> must explain to the people of America. Until the implications
> of this are clear to them, there will be no appreciation either
> now or in the days ahead of the stand our country will take
> in important issues. [3]

This very last piece of advice that Gandhiji (the suffix
"ji" is one of the commonest additions to a name in India,
conveying an idea of respect, and applied indiscriminately to
all kinds of people—men, women, boys and children. Gandhi
himself preferred the addition of "ji" rather than the use of the
title, "Mahatma") gave Mrs. Pandit, after her assignment as

Ambassador to America was announced, is at once the key to
the national mood as well as the criterion of judgment for international issues. The purity of means is set above the ends themselves: and attainment of the ends is none too easy. The
people ask for bread; and the Communists promise that. They
want security from fear of foreign invasion: the national faith
would not compromise to the point of adopting a partisan
stand in the Cold War. Ideological aspirations may appear to
be of secondary importance in the time of primeval necessity;
hunger would refuse to bide its time till the purity of means
are established. The invisible fortress of non-violence has yet
to prove its invincibility: how can you fight tanks and tor-
pedoes with love and tolerance?

Two important features of Indian thinking are its historic
outlook and its idealist nature.

Norman Cousins, Editor of the *Saturday Review,* made an
admirable summary of the Asian mood in his preface to a long
record of his latest interviews with the Prime Ministers of
India and Pakistan:

> Our frame of reference in the world of today is the Cold
> War; the Asian frame of reference is the experience of the
> past two centuries. Thus, there is a natural and threatening
> division between the contemporary and the historical in the
> outlook of both areas. [4]

These historic and idealistic elements run right through
the entire system of Indian thinking; political issues can
claim little immunity from this orientation. Gandhiji once
said that even God does not dare to appear before a starving
man except in the form of food. Will non-violence and pure
ideals give one food? Or will they be used as an opiate to
perpetuate inequalities of income and opportunity?

Flayed alive by these simple but substantial questions,
the poor peasant would mutely question the point and purpose in the achievement of a Republican status for India in the
community of nations. But the orientation of his thinking has

roots deeper than the disturbances of scepticism. His historic perspective does not urge him to see red in Communism. Invasion by successive armies, conquest by different nations, and occupation by dissimilar races over the ages, makes a nation less receptive to the suggestions of change by an infant idea, born in the backwash of the Second World War. Cataclysmic changes in the form and organization of the different territories are too familiar to evoke any startling effects. Life flows at an even ebb, people are hardly ever in a hurry, a sense of eternal existence brings a comforting calm to the nerves which makes the people less liable to exitation.

Turn to the immediate past: it speaks of the association of India with the West. All memories are not entirely pleasant and Indian memories of the last two centuries are not the sweetest of its recorded past. To quote Toynbee:

> India's experience with the West has thus been more painful and more humiliating than China's or Turkey's, and much more so than Russia's or Japan's; but just for this reason, it has been also much more intimate . . . On the surface, those Hindus who have adopted our, to them, extremely alien western culture in the areas of technology and science, language and literature, administration and law, appear to have been more successful than the Russians in harmonizing with their native way of life, a western way that is intrinsically more alien to them than it is to the Russians. Yet the *tension in the Hindu soul must* be extreme, and sooner or later must find some means of *discharging* itself. [5] (Italics supplied)

Superimposed on this surcharged tension created by westernization is the tempting bait of material alleviation by the Communists and the idealist addiction to non-violence. It may not be fashionable to suggest that non-violent means will ward off the modern barbarity of global warfare: but neither would have been the affirmation that independence for a fifth of the world's population could be attained without war or violence of any serious degree, India's unique accomplishment. It is now history that Gandhiji, the "Father of the Nation," led India to the goal of Swaraj (Self-Government) through non-violence. And that which was won by non-violence can be kept by non-violence. To feel that a nation is fighting for eternal values should impart to it a supreme calm which should disabuse its mind from the scramble for power and prestige in the international sphere. However, it is perfect love that casts out fear, and in politics, as in life, perfection is not easy. Therefore, there is on the one hand, the urge to draw on the sublime calm which arises from idealism; on the other, the call to political expediency. The immediate issues cry for speedy solutions which sometimes destroy the poise of the wider frame. These temporary imbalances stand out in the eyes of an observant world, which is involuntarily set in opposition to an alien system of thinking with a frame of reference stretching out from the abyss of the past, and peering into the unborn future. Misreading is easy; the apparent moral superiority is assumed. For, to the world, it is not easy to understand how the absence of adequate defenses could leave a country without anxiety; how the portent of present danger can almost be ineffective in driving it into defensive alliances and armament. The reason is that the experiment is unique; and eternal misunderstanding is the price of uniqueness.

It is in this context of strong cultural tension, violent economic conditioning and uniquely misunderstood idealism that American Aid to India is set.

The lines between economic and political differences merge more or less imperceptibly in the region of communism; for communism is both a political and an economic institution. Therefore, views on the biggest votary of the Communist economic system which is also the biggest political institution of that setup, tends to be simultaneously political and economic. In other words, a vote for or against Russia has implications in both the economic and political spheres. This is all the more intriguing because the merging of shades is not always borne in mind in international parleys. As a result of this, it is not infrequently that a non-readiness to condemn outrightly every little move that Soviet Russia makes is interpreted as an implied approval of their economic system as well.

The awakening of a nation is a time-consuming process; but when it finally does awake, problems of emancipation are raised which have remained hidden for centuries. In India, for instance, the people, in the wake of freedom, discovered that they were hungry. And hunger needs sufficient food. In the struggle for existence primeval needs and their satiation tend to acquire altogether too high a significance. This almost natural order of priorities may include a hasty generalization about all that the renascent nation is trying to do. In the case of India, it will bear repetition to say that the material is not the end-all of existence; nor is the national tempo set in terms of the things that people possess. The views on a nation that struggles not to live by bread alone, but which certainly wants to eat bread, have been heavily colored to outside observers by the context of their own nation's setting in world history and international politics. Maturity of political vision and the sense of history appears to be allowed to suffer occasional lapses in judgments on India. For instance, one of the leading theologians in the United States, Reinhold Niebuhr, who has been accused of being more socially alive to the material needs of people than current concepts of the lines of demarcation between theology and sociology would warrant, discusses the Christian attitude towards communism. In his article on the subject, he discusses the Christian and other approaches to the problem, including that of India's non-Christian Prime Minister Nehru. Pointing out that "we face two problems in our generation rather than one: the avoidance of war and resistance to tyranny," he observes that the "pure" idealists are always tempted either to war against communism in the name of justice, or to come to terms with it in the name of peace. India's attitude towards communism is an uncommitted position, while the United States takes a committed position. Reinhold Niebuhr gives a left-handed compliment when he says:

> The ideals of these contrasting idealists may be purer than ours. We cannot claim greater moral purity; but perhaps we may claim to possess a wisdom which is more relevant to our two-pronged predicament. [6]

Disturbing thoughts assail one's mind when a leading Christian thinker apparently chooses to evaluate an ideological position in terms of the immediate and the prudent. If a frenzy of "practicality" were to declare that the only tenable position in the international situation is one of commitment, and "wise" commitment at that, the people in India would have to think twice about it. For, the wisdom of the ages does not sanction a too ready and unceremonious jump to a cut-and-dry pronouncement on a none-too-simple situation. India may not be hypersensitive to the expansionist design of the successors of the Czars, but it is vitally involved in feeding its people *without* sacrificing its soul for any mess of pottage.

> Nehru said that history had selected India as one of democracy's chief testing grounds. This was a contest which he and India welcomed, a challenge which must be met head on. Can a poverty-stricken country recently emerged from colonialism maintain and expand freedom while it organizes and develops its economic resources? The Communists say this cannot be done and should not be tried, but India disagrees. [7]

When alliance of any form is a rejected premise, mud-slinging by any human system against any other is not the best way to promote either understanding or co-operation. The Master condemned sin; but He also loved the sinner. Condemn by all means, the materialistic basis of Communism; but let it not be overlooked for a moment that the common man turns and sees speedy succor in Robin Hoods while the arms of the law are shrouded in the dignified trappings of supine inactivity.

It is greatly gratifying to note that influential voices in the United States are not entirely ignorant in their attitude towards issues which are vital to India. It is heartening that the General Council of the Presbyterian Churches of the United States of America approved unanimously the letter prepared by their Council on Communism. Three little words in that document appear to crystalize the essence of the historic insight, prophetic vision, and Christian concern of the author of that letter, Dr. John A. Mackay.

Communism, to our sorrow, is wedded to a philosophy of lying. [8]

There is condemnation of sin: here a saving condemnation, because there is the simultaneous concern about an erring brother fallen on evil ways.

Law and opinion are considered to be the safeguards of democracy. Good opinion is based on correct information. The differences in the views and interpretations mentioned above are not abysmal, although they are threateningly serious. The differences loom larger against a background of an America eager to be friendly to India, and an India eager to be friendly to America. When the soothing balm of true information is applied to the uncomfortable joints of the body of cooperative international life in order to realize the beauty of the democratic way of life, the differences will emerge in their proper perspective.

PART II

Production Problems

CHAPTER THREE

ORIENTATION TO ALTERNATIVES

"Produce or Perish" is a slogan popular in India. The slogan is clear, but it does cover a multitude of uncertainties and ambivalence, almost to the point of counterbalancing the certainty of the slogan.

"Well, we have done it; why can't they do it?" is an attitude of mind that seems to color most Western judgments on India. If Western Europe could bring down her birthrate, which at one time was nearly double that of the present Indian birthrate, it would seem reasonable to the West to expect the solution to the population problem of India within this generation, now that efficient methods of birth control are available. In regard to agricultural production, intensive and extensive cultivations in vogue in the West would seem to indicate the solution to the food problem of India. While atomic energy is seen as accessible mainly to occidental nations, they feel justified in expecting their oriental counterparts to make more rapid strides in their industrial production with at least electric energy.

It is still true that one can take a horse to the water, but twenty cannot make it drink. One implicit assumption in the expectations of the West for rapid progress in Indian production problems—population, agricuultural and industrial—is a certain amount of automation of operations. The avail-

31

ability of birth control techniques, for instance, is assumed to indicate their immediate use. The advantages of different methods of cultivation are taken as reason enough for the immediate application of same. But the going is not quite so smooth. There seems to be need for adjustment—adjustment between the human and the machine components of production.

The need for adjustment is self-evident, but the process of adjustment is not equally obvious. The search for an appropriate process will constitute the burden of inquiry in Part II.

The population of India will be about 750,000,000 by the 1980's unless some drastic curtailment of the birthrate or increment in the deathrate intervenes between now and then. The sheer size of India's population can create perceptible repercussions in the industrial nations of the West because 750 million consumers demanding food and clothing can affect the price of food and raw materials in the international market. If raw materials become costly, the prices of manufactures will correspondingly increase. Higher prices of manufactured goods can force industrialized nations to alter their plans of production, particularly when the convenience of assured markets in colonial possessions or dominion territories is not available.

Or, if the vast population were to voice its discontent with the existing distribution of the world's resources, it would come as an economic sequel to the political democracy that has been established, in varying degrees, in many countries. Fomentation by communism may not even be necessary to fan the flames of hunger-born revolutions.

With these unpleasant possibilities, the use by India of effective measures to control her population growth assumes fresh weight and significance.

"Baby or new car?" is a consideration that presupposes the existence in the mind of the decisionmaker, some product which may be roughly as desirable as a baby. To the majority of Indian peasants this alternative does not exist. The high infant mortality prevalent in India until recent times, when it declined to about 150 per 1,000, necessitated a large number of births to insure the survival of a few. That at least one of them be a son is strongly institutionalized. Religious customs of the majority of the people in India bring about this institutionalization. Since it is easier to control death than birth, the impact of health measures is an immediate addition to the population. If birth control measures should succeed, they should be shown to be germane to the mores and customs of India.

Agricultural production stifles under the wastefully small size of the plots of land. How can the plots be consolidated is an important question. The force of tradition may tend to outweigh the advantages of improved production. However, persuasion to improve may not be out of the bounds of possibility.

Industrial production calls for some degree of dehumanization to ensure efficiency. Diligent attention to machine production calls for a sense of time, metronome—like accuracy, and an impersonal relationship between the machine and the operator. These are bound to grate with the family-oriented sense of "belongingness," but a gradual initiation may gain acceptance if the deeper sociological values are not undermined in the process.

With this brief mapping of broad outlines, a closer examination of the mind of India in relation to production problems—population, agricultural and industrial—may now be attempted.

CHAPTER FOUR

POPULATION AND POSSIBILITIES

Human welfare and consumption levels—declining mortality and increasing population in India—religious position with reference to birth control—verbalization without action—limitation: an unfamiliar concept—recreation by procreation—birth control measures in India—government efforts at birth control—prospects of birth control in India.

MANPOWER HAS ASSUMED unprecedented importance in the twentieth century. Its high potential value was recognized afresh during the post World War II days when it had to be put into cold storage. Coal, if not extracted today, can be extracted tomorrow or the day after. But today's ability to work cannot be used tomorrow. This is the curse of unemployment in any form—voluntary, frictional, seasonal or involuntary. When a country is designated as underemployed or underdeveloped, one of the implications is that the labor power in that country is not exploited to the extent that is possible under given technical conditions.

To an extent which might have seemed inconceivable even fifty years ago, there has come increasing recognition that 2,400 million people have somehow to contrive to live together, and share together the resources of the earth; that the general impoverishment of any area is a matter of concern to all areas; and that the technical experience and knowledge acquired in rapidly changing industrialized societies have somehow to be made available to those communities that are less advanced and less well-equipped. That this has come to pass is an historical and inspiring fact. Indeed, it has been suggested by a distinguished historian that in the broad sweep the 20th century will be chiefly remembered in future centuries not as an age of political conflicts or technical inventions, but as an age in which human society dared to think of the welfare of the whole human race as a practical objective."[1]

1112193

"The welfare of the whole human race" suggests the utilitarian maxim, "the greatest good of the greatest number," which number, the cynic would say, is one. Whatever be the actual number, the concept is important: should there be a large number with a low level of living, or a smaller number with a high level of living?

One criterion for deciding the optimum population of a country is the resources available for the population. The standard of consumption maintainable would be an index of this availability. The estimated energy and protein content of the national average of food supplies per capita in India and the United States were as follows:[2]

TABLE I [2]

CONSUMPTION LEVELS—

INDIA AND THE UNITED STATES OF AMERICA

(1)	(2) Calories Number per day	(3) Total Protein grams per day	(4) Animal Protein grams per day
Prewar			
India	1970	56	8
U.S.A.	3150	89	50
1949–50			
India	1620	42	6
U.S.A.	3170	91	61
1950–51			
India	1570	42	6
U.S.A.	3210	92	61

Less than a tenth of the animal protein and less than half of the total protein intake of the American average obviously cannot provide equivalent nourishment to the average Indian. Two alternative methods of increasing the average level of consumption would be: either to raise the resources available for consumption, or to decrease the number of people to be fed.

Regarding the increase of food supply, the First Five Year Plan has a fairly decent record of cereal production. With a total production of 54.3 million tons and an estimated population of 378 million, the per capita availability of cereal in India in 1954-55 worked out to 14.4ounces which is 0.5 higher than the balanced diet laid down by the Nutrition Advisory Committee.[3] It also exceeded the target set for the end of the First Five Year Plan, i.e., 13.71 ounces per head for 1955-56.

It is gratifying to note that cereal production has progressed according to schedule. But this still does not alter substantially the picture of inadequate animal and total protein intake per day.

The sea can be a source of food for India.

In 1948, fish landings in India were estimated at 0.52 million tons of which 71 per cent was from the sea and the rest from inland waters. This works out to an annual per capita availability of 3.4 pounds in India against 16 pounds in Ceylon, 70 in Burma and 90 in Japan. With 15 million acres of inland water area and 2,900 miles of coast line the possibilities of sea as a source of food are not inconsiderable.

Thus, cereal production and seafood potentials seem to constitute the more important entries on the credit side of the first alternative, viz., to increase the average level of consumption.

The other alternative, decreasing the number of people to be fed, may be conceived in terms of either killing people or preventing their birth.

Dismissing the first procedure as unworthy of consideration, the second may be dealt with in some detail. It should be observed that there is no question of reducing the number of people nor is it even one of decreasing the present growth of population: it is only a matter of arresting the increasing rate of growth. Even if India were to stop adding annually 13 per 1,000 to her population of about 378 million, she would still have to face two grim aspects of her population problem; namely, size and density.

India, merely by stopping the growth of its population, will not be released from her population problem. The present generation of India has inherited the population problem. Even if they get rid of the growth, the ratio of people to its resources is already very high there. But the only moral I draw from all this is: let us be very sympathetic with their needs; let us recognize all the obstacles they face, which the English did not face in 1800, which Western Europe did not face, which Sweden did not face in 1870 when it began its great progress, which Canada and the United States never had to face—the problem of beginning with a serious handicap of population density. [4]

The population of India is increasing by four and a half millions every year—the increase during the past ten years is equal to the entire population of France.

This increase is likely to be generously aided by the improvement of health brought about by measures ranging from cleaner wells in villages to anti-tubercular vaccination. Every year, more than 500,000 people in India die of tuberculosis while many more may be suffering from the malady. The present progress of anti-tubercular vaccination may indicate a successful measure of combating tuberculosis. Plague, which claimed 500 out of every 100,000 persons in 1907 (registered deaths in British India), evidenced the most spectacular decline among the three epidemic diseases universally recognizable in India. Virtual elimination of this disease in the near future is not unlikely. Smallpox and cholera, the other two universally noted epidemics in India, are slower in their decline but the fact of their decline itself is established.

The progress in medical research and sanitary habits of the people increases the number of survivors in different age groups. These measures also lower the mortality rate among infants. A proportion of the infants thus surviving would be females, and when they grow up, they in turn contribute to further additions to the population.

In the Census Report for India for 1941 an examination was made of the saving of life in sofar as only the reduction of infant mortality was concerned. The effect of such infant survivors on the future growth of India's population was investigated. It was shown that if the trend in infant mortality rate continued at the same rate as in the past there would be on this account alone an addition of the order of 7 million persons in 1951, e.g., the increase alone would exceed the total population of the island of Ceylon. For the same reason, the addition in 1961 was estimated to be 13.3 million, i.e., almost as large as the total population of Argentina.

The partition of the country in 1947 has necessitated that revised estimates of such accretions to population be made for the areas now comprising the Union of India and that the vital statistical data of recent years, especially those affected by famines and the war or post-war conditions, be also taken into account. . . .

It is (therefore) likely that the decline in infant mortality which has occured during the period 1920-1946 would alone have added approximately 2.5 millions to the population of the Union of India by the year 1941, i.e., as much as the total population of Ireland.

Looking ahead, if it is postulated that the decline in infant mortality will continue at the same rate as during the period 1920-1946, the addition to population by the census year of 1951 on account of the survivorship of infants alone is likely to be about 5.5 millions and in 1961 about 10.3 millions. In other words reduction in infant mortality alone will have resulted in 1961, in the addition to India of a population of the same dimensions as that of the dominion of Canada. [5]

These studies bring home in no uncertain terms the need for restricting births in India. This effort will be directed towards arresting the rate of growth of the population.

But, in tackling this problem, the general awareness of the problem itself is not extremely helpful. Women in India are not exactly crying out for birth control. In a dumb, vague way, the majority of them would desire to escape the drudgery of child births. But one foreigner observer expressed the view that most of these women would be "shocked by the very thought of contraception." [6] Twenty years later, this view is not totally irrelevant to the Indian situation. "The "shock" at the very thought of contraception does not seem to stem from any religious injunction or fear of probable unhealthy results for the potential mother.

The positions of the major religions of India as regards birth control are as follows: HINDUISM: Celibacy is advocated in the sacred writings of Hinduism, but this is a cult of life for the elite. Celibacy is considered to imply far more than mere abstinence from sexual union. Its value lay in the positive attributes of life devoted to higher pursuits pertaining to the mind, made possible by the renunciation of normal sex-life. The tenets of Hinduism recognize four stages in a man's life, the second of which is *Grahasthāshrama*. Each *āshrama* is a stage of life, a sequence of effort, and *Graha* is home. Thus, the setting up of a home is mandatory for the Hindu and he must have a successor, a son, to light his funeral pyre to enable him to make the transition from one life to another marked by death.

While a son is more or less mandatory for the fulfilment of one's life, the Hindu Scriptures do not seem to say anything against birth control. In fact, the *Brihad Aranyak Upanishad* describes a manner of marital relations which does not result in conception. Prescriptions for the use of salves and the drinking of potions in order to avoid pregnancies are also available in other Sanskrit writings of early days.

ISLAM: According to Imam El Ghazaly, who was a great authority on Islamic philosophy, and to other reliable sources, birth control is allowed in Islam in cases of poverty and for other social considerations. Imam El Ghazaly even said that women could adopt birth control as a means of maintaining their beauty. This reference was brought up by Dr. Mohammed Awad Mohammed of Alexandria University early in 1954, when he was replying to another rector of the University who was reported to have stated that birth control violated Islamic principles.

CHRISTIANITY: Perhaps one of the earliest mentions of birth control in the Bible is that of Onan:

> And Onan knew that the seed should not be his; and it came to pass when he went in unto his brother's wife, that he spilled it on the ground, lest that he should give seed to his brother. [7]

It would be safe to say that Christianity, as a religion, has not yet made any strong case against birth control. Those who oppose the Roman Catholic position against birth control point out that birth control measures, mostly contraceptive in nature, aim at preventing the formation of life and not the destruction of it afterwards. Also, they point out that if the Roman Church would approve of the rhythm method of control, the essence of interference with the unrestricted sexual union is accepted: which acceptance would reduce the issue of contraception to a matter of mere mechanics.

The Vatican's objection to family limitation does not seem to be without qualifications. Reverend Father Stanislaus de Lestapōs, official Vatican delegate to the United Nations' World Population Conference at Rome in September, 1954, told the conference that governments in underdeveloped countries with high birth rates have a duty to carry on propaganda in favor of reducing births.[8] These governments should inform citizens of the consequences of overpopulation, Reverend Father de Lestapōs declared. Married couples who heed the warnings and limit the size of their families are worthy of imitation, he said.

Thus, in India, religious opposition to birth control is not anticipated, at least not in any considerable degree. This statement is highly significant in regard to a nation where religious sanction to human activity is highly institutionalized as a necessary prerequisite.

It would be odd to be actively interested in something and then to sit tight in a corner doing nothing about it. A keen awareness of a thing to be accomplished is expected to bring about concrete action. This, however, is not necessarily a logical sequence in India: not in sofar as the subject of birth control is concerned at any rate.

A number of surveys indicate that the people are in favor of birth control. But the count of people who use birth control regularly reveals that the large majority of those who register themselves as being favorable to birth control is far greater than the number actually taking appropriate measures.

The Gokhale Institute of Politics and Economics in Poona, with the help of the Rockefeller Foundation, established a Section in Demography and Population Studies in 1951. A report on the data collected in Poona City and in 5 towns and 30 villages in Poona District was published in February, 1954, by V. M. Dandekar and Kumudini Dandekar of the Demography Section.

Amongst the city-dwellers of 850 persons questioned as to whether or not they practiced any contraceptive method, 76 persons answered in the affirmative. Of the remainder, 14 knew about contraception, but did not practice it; 509 knew absolutely nothing about it; and 251 indicated that the question did not concern them. Dandekar observes:

The most significant fact about the situation is the large number of persons, both male and female, in the city as well as in the non-city area, who said that they would welcome information on the subject of family limitation and the substantial number among them who voluntarily said that they would immediately adopt the methods in practice. [9]

Similar desire to limit family size was expressed in the Attitude Survey conducted in 1953 among about 800 couples from Bangalore City, Mysore State, and about 300 from rural areas. A fertility study conducted by the All-India Institute of Hygiene and Public Health among some selected groups of the population of Calcutta also indicated a desire for limited family. Yet in both Mysore and Calcutta the gap between the number of children actually born and the number desired is equally wide—5.4 against 3. The Attitude Survey conducted in the Lodi Colony in New Delhi, which is a housing project to serve junior Government Civil Servants of the Central Secretariat, in May, 1952, also revealed a vocalized interest in family limitation.

In this context of vocalized but unrealized interest, Chandrasekaran's observations may be noted. It may be recalled that he was the expert appointed by the Technical Assistance Administration of the United Nations to carry out pilot studies on the rhythm method of family planning in India. In the course of his address to the Second All India Conference on Family Planning held in Lucknow in January, 1955, Chandrasekaran said:

In spite of an overwhelming desire to limit family size, the practice of family limitation was extremely limited. Less than 3 per cent of couples in the rural area and about 10 per cent in Bangalore City had adopted methods of family limitation, most of them by means of abstinence. Knowledge of methods of family limitation was equally restricted. In the rural areas 90 per cent of women and 85 per cent of men had no knowledge of family limitation. In Bangalore City the women who had no knowledge varied from 52 to 73 per cent in the four strata selected for survey. Among men, 51 to 77 per cent in the different strata had no knowledge of the methods. It was also significant that the method best known in both urban and rural areas was sterilization of the women. Next in importance was sterilization of the husband, followed by "condom" in the rural area. Knowledge of coitus-interruptus was extremely meagre. [10]

If the support of the idea of birth control remains by and large purely verbal, it seems to indicate the need for exploration on a deeper level.

When it is suggested that the average Indian does not have any concept of limitation, it does not mean that he is not bound by the division of day and night into hours and minutes and seconds. Physically he is, but psychically he is not.

During the 1951 census, when a census enumerator asked an old lady her age, she said, "30." Whereupon the enumerator pointed out that her daughter was 25. The old lady said, "Oh, then it is 120." Whether the arithmetic average of 30 and 120 would have any meaning at all is a relatively minor consideration in the light of the concept of time that the old lady indicated. To her, thirty and one hundred and twenty are just equally indifferent numbers.

The farmer's day has only a few hours in it: six o'clock, ten o'clock, four o'clock, evening, midnight. These "hours" are merely used as indicators of the broad sweep of daylight or moonlight within which some event took place. In other words, *the hour is an ordinal and not cardinal concept.*

An unhurried approach to life that defies analysis and an unconcern that baffles ordinary codes of conduct naturally presents considerable problems to birth control methods which employ the idea of limitation. For instance, consider the rhythm method. According to this method, a woman has to take (or have taken) her vaginal temperature daily for six months before her own personal "safe-period" can be determined. To a people for whom time moves in infinite cycles, daily temperatures for six months would simply grate with their mores and habits. The religion of the majority of the population teaches them that life is an eternal thing, and that mortal life is but a single span in the ever-rotating wheel of life. Death is only the beginning of another life whose nature depends on what was done with one's life before death. The primary concern is to get out of the woes of the wheel of life, which calls for saintly living. All other issues pale to insignificance before this towering target and supreme concern of life. This target itself has no limitation in time and space, which means that nothing else in the ordinary business of mankind can claim any successful subdivision of indivisable eternity either.

Limitation is an alien concept not only in the realm of time but also in the realm of resources. The means of an average Indian are definitely limited; the national income per capita is about one-fortieth that of the American. But let there come a guest to the home, and the poorest peasant becomes a prince of hospitality. The host himself would drink water but the guest must have milk. Hospitality is so institutionalized that it was quite possible for those who came as merchants to remain as rulers. This trait of hospitality is something more than mere courtesy; it almost becomes a component of the outlook on life, both on the personal and the national scale.

The pertinence of this trait to family limitation considerations lies in the fact that the average Indian does not have any adequate sense of his own limitation in means of livelihood. As a consequence of this attitude, the poverty of the masses seems to make no impression whatsoever on their manner of living. Even though the peasant has only half his requirement of rice, he would not cut down on any of his celebrations: perhaps they are an escape mechanism. Even though he cannot afford it, he must have the biggest ceremonies possible for the weddings of his sons and daughters. He would find the largest dowry possible for his daughter, and then continue to over-extend himself in the purchase of the ornaments and gifts and other embellishments. All this would sound fantastic to those who are used to prudent calculations. But it adds up to the simple, and somewhat startling fact that the Indian does not act in full cognizance of his poverty: he does not realize his limitations in terms of worldly possessions and means of livelihood.

If the head of the household does not pause to think whether or not he has enough provisions at home to treat his guest, but rather spares no pains to accord a most royal welcome to any guest, calculations of a higher order may not be a fair demand. The cost of a baby is certainly a calculation involving more dimensions than those involved in treating a guest who may stay for a couple of meals. The baby not only stays for a far greater number of meals but also widens his needs in terms of education, equipment and opportunity as the days go by. Corresponding to the increasing demands, there will be the father's non-increasing ability to provide for the baby. But none of these simple truths ever enter the minds of the peasant couple who unite to produce a baby and bow mutely to the inviolable decree of fate.

The virtual absence of recreation in the lives of both the agricultural and the industrial worker of India is generally overlooked. The wheel of life is not only eternal and ever-rotating but also monotonous. Monotony can be sickening. And a sickening feeling of the body may urge people to seek stimulation. Physical thrills provided at home would be most inexpensive and so procreation becomes a form of recreation. Thus there is the vicious circle of sickening monotony, physical indulgence, more children, sickening monotony, etc. The progeny is not likely to be blest with abounding vitality either: They are already heirs to the atmosphere unsatiated cravings that in part led to their very creation. These unwanted by-products of the futile search for recreation come under the unconscious spell of meagre means. Thus children who ought to be a blessing become a millstone: a weary care loaded on an aching back.

The proud blossoms of the morrow will be cherished and reared as priceless leaders when material problems cease to squeeze the joy and color out of living. In order to bring this about, at least two changes will be called for: one, the parents should be able to enjoy recreational facilities; and two, their sense of time must be modified.

It might not be overemphasizing to say that the parents should be able to *enjoy* recreational facilities. For, enjoyment of recreation implies an orientation to relaxation. Emotionally, the Indian farmer or industrial worker will have little difficulty in relaxing. But his access to means of enjoyment is strictly limited. However, it is gratifying to note the possibilities of close-circuit television in the rural areas of India. One plan is to introduce mobile TV units which could bring the eyes and ears of the world to the doors of the villages. William S. Halstead, president of Unitel, Inc., a global-television enterprise, is currently working on an international television relay network joining the free nations of the world. The idea has been endorsed by the Senate Foreign Relations Commitee on Overseas Information Programs; the United States Congress has authorized a Commission on Governmental use of International Telecommunications.

Halstead's plan is to use TV beams with a range of 300 miles (by means of new relay methods) over a global path, starting from New York and going through Canada, across Greenland and Iceland, on to Scotland via the Faeroes and Shetland Islands, then across Europe, Southern Asia and Pacific islands to Japan, and across the Pacific via the various island groups to San Francisco. The advantage of this global path is that at no place on the path is there more than 290 miles between land masses.

India is considering Halstead's plan to erect its first TV station at Allahabad. Its programs will be devoted almost exclusively to education, including teaching the population in the outlying villages to read and write. Ultimately a TV network may serve all India. Professor Humayun Kabir, India's Secretary of Education, says, "We fully expect that television will advance the cultural level of rural India by 500 years." [11]

It may not be stretching the point too far to suggest that at present the peasant who is prepared to be outgoing is driven to introversion because there is no interesting external point on which to focus his thoughts and attention. He sees the same sights, hears the same sounds and therefore does the same things all the year round. Give him a chance to have some glimpse of the panoramic world outside his own village; let him have at least a passing chance to acquaint himself with the advancement of modern techniques; allow him at least a few minutes of relaxation when he can transport himself to distant lands and different surroundings: Then the present introversion, almost verging on the neurotic, will start to yield place to his truer extrovertish nature.

The changing of the concept of time will be a lengthy process. It is one thing to use a watch and another to have a sense of time. The peasant does have a good sense of time, but its dimensions are in seasons or months, while birth control calls for a disposition to keep track of the seconds. Payment by the hour and overtime pay in industry may be helpful in making the worker time-conscious. Part-time jobs for the peasant for which payment will be by the hour and graded by results, may be a good beginning in the drive for time-consciousness among the masses.

Kingsley Davis and Judith Blake have made an elaborate list of the factors entering into social structure and fertility.[12] It may be recalled that Davis wrote a comprehensive volume on the population of India and Pakistan; therefore, his analysis of the general social factors affecting fertility may be particularly relevant to consideration of the possibilities of birth control measures in India.

Birth control by mechanical and chemical means, rhythm, simulated intercourse without penetration, etc. is listed under factors affecting exposure to conception. Other measures like sterilization, subincision also pertain to fecundity or infecundity as affected by voluntary causes.

These measures are not as yet popular in India.

Perhaps the most important institutionalized measure affecting births in India is the period of lactation which enforces not voluntary but involuntary abstinence. The wife in the village goes home to her family of origin during the seventh month of pregnancy and returns only around the sixth month after delivery of the child. Generally speaking, while factors governing exposure to conception *during* intercourse are regulated in the West, in India, the usual measure taken in rural areas is abstinence from intercourse during the period of lactation.

Among the factors governing the formation and dissolution of unions during the reproductive period, is the legal age for marriage which has now been raised by means of legislation to 18 for boys and 16 for girls. While this postpones legal union, the number of potential children so reduced is perhaps compensated for by the decrease of wasteful unions before maturity, which is possible under an early marriage age for boys and girls. Permanent celibacy is almost inactive as a factor governing formation of unions during the reproductive period: not more than 6 per cent of the women are unmarried by the time they are in their early twenties. Therefore, the only practical restraints are afforded by the lactation period, and cultural and religious taboos on intercourse during certain times of the year. The dependence of the people on foetal mortality, and similar factors affecting gestation and successful parturition, for birth regulation is admittedly more dangerous and probably less dependable. But Margaret Sanger started her inquiry into the factors affecting exposure to conception through her own personal attempts at preventing childbirth during gestation. This may indicate that if India shows a preparedness to limit the family at the gestation stage, she may be induced to go one step farther and to try to work on factors affecting conception.

The Health Survey and Development Committee in its Report (1947) discussed the question of population. Subsequently the Planning Commission, in its Outline Plan (1951), put forward a tentative family planning program. The United Nations, the World Health Organization, and a number of visiting experts contributed their share to the thinking on the subject and formulation of programs. The 1951 Census Report further focused attention on the problem. The program was finalized as part of the Five-Year Plan in 1952. Two committees, the Population Policy Committee and the Family Planning Research and Programs Committee, were constituted. The latter committee considered the subject and made recommendations which formed the basis of the Indian Government's action in the matter. The main recommendation of the committee was in regard to the development of family planning programs as an integral part of maternal and child health services and of health services in general.

The implementation of the proposals, however, has been proceeding very slowly. The Family Planning Research and Programs Committee, in its meeting held on 14-16th April, 1955, in New Delhi, passed a resolution which said:

The Family Planning Research and Programs Committee has noted with grave concern the extremely slow progress made in the implementation of its proposals. From its first meeting in July 1953 onwards the Committee has been anxious to promote the expansion of family planning services as quickly as possible. The Committee was given to understand that there were only about 165 family planning centers in the country and that many of them functioned at a low level of efficiency. Therefore the Committee urged, at this and subsequent meetings, that . . . The Family Planning Research and Programs Committee should be made an autonomous body so that family planning activities and studies into various aspects of the population problem may be developed on a broad basis with as little delay as possible. . . .

An outlay of 101.47 million Rupees ($20.92 million) has been recommended by the Director General of Health Services during 1956-61 under the second Five-Year Plan. The various components of the outlay are as follows:·

TABLE 2 [13]

PROPOSED OUTLAY ON BIRTHCONTROL MEASURES
DURING THE SECOND FIVE-YEAR PLAN 1956-61

(1)		(2) 1956-57	(3) 1957-58	(4) 1958-59	(5) 1959-60	(6) 1960-61	(7) Total
1. Subsidies to States for opening of Family Planning Clinics	NR	$ 69,290	$ 69,290	$ 69,290	$ 69,290	$ 68,000	$ 345,160
	R	1,402,070	2,630,900	3,744,330	4,569,100	5,383,500	17,729,900
2. Training Program	NR	395,250	207,635	1,445	1,445	1,445	607,220
	R	33,815	36,705	132,165	183,715	235,250	621,650
3. Education for Family Planning	NR	582,470	......	......	......	......;	582,470
	R	171,750	120,210	85,980	......	......	377,940
4. Research Program	NR	......	......	......	......	......	......,
	R	103,092	103,092	103,092	103,092	103,092	515,460
5. Control Organization	NR	......	......	......	......	......	55,660
	R	17,320	17,320	17,320	17,320	17,320	86,600
Total	NR	$1,102,680	$ 276,910	$ 70,720	$ 70,720	$ 69,480	$ 1,590,510
	R	1,728,035	2,908,250	4,082,890	4,873,200	5,739,175	19,331,550
							$20,922,060
State Govt.		$ 150,725	$ 493,200	$ 934,430	$1,718,350	$2,414,225	$ 5,710,930

NR—Non-Recurring   R—Recurring

PHYSICAL TARGETS:

1. Family Planning Centers 5,558 (to be opened by Central Government).
   2,790 (to be opened by State authorities).
2. Training and Research Institute.
3. Contraceptive Testing Center.
4. Training Centers in States, 10.
5. Publicity vans, 100.

TABLE 3 [14]

PERSONNEL REQUIREMENTS FOR FAMILY PLANNING

(1)	(2)	(3)	(4)	(5)
		Trained		
	Medical	Social		Sanitary
Year	Officers	Workers	Nurses	Inspectors
1956-57	231	1230	226	364
1957-58	226	1228	224	340
1958-59	226	1228	224	340
1959-60	226	1228	224	340
1960-61	222	1224	220	334
Total	1131	6138	1118	1718

What does all this add up to? Is India actually doing something to control the increase of her population?

P. K. Whelpton, who travelled through 60 countries in the last 32 years to study the population problems, had the following to say on the question:

> In some of the states and cities, quite a little work has been done toward getting family-planning centers established and operating. The Central Government has been laying the ground for a large-scale operation, rather than actually getting it started. On the basis of some information I have received recently, this may change quite rapidly within a few months. The Central Government may get back of some large-scale tests of how to spread family planning among the masses of the population in certain areas, using foam tablets as the method. [15]

In view of the relative immobility of attitude towards the concept of limitation, it would seem that social pressure must be exerted as a concerted measure along with the process of making available efficient and inexpensive contraceptives.

The concept of "critical minimum effort" [16] is a valuable theoretical structure in the context of the present Indian situation. India is experiencing a faster decline in mortality than in natality. It has been the experience of Western European countries that in the transition from high birth and death rates to low birth and death rates, death rates fall faster than birth rates. The increasing pressure of population as a consequence of the decline in death rate preceding the decline in birth rate in India has been discussed previously. The "critical minimum effort thesis" states that the effort made to achieve a change from an underdeveloped equilibrium must be of a certain minimum magnitude in order to result in a lasting improvement in the level of living. Otherwise, whatever gains are made will at best be temporary.

In the process of exploring the practical measures of implementing the principle, it appears that one of the best methods for impressing the minds of the laborers with the imperativeness of family limitations is through the exercise of social pressure. One means suggested is housing built for four-member families. When one lives in an area where everybody else has only two children social pressure may induce a corresponding limitation of one's own family.

Whatever the mechanics of bringing about family limitation in India, the program must take adequate note of the fact that there may be the slip 'twixt the cup and the lip; between the availability of efficient contraceptives and the drop of birth rates from the current 40 to say 26.5 per 1,000 in order to offset the effect of probable death rate reduction in the next 10 years by 13.5 per 1,000. Safeguards against slips are called for in the nature of measures aimed at not merely educating the people in the techniques of family limitation but also in demonstrating to them that the philosophy behind such limitation is congenial to the philosophy of their own living.

AGRICULTURE—A WAY OF LIFE

Population and land resources—why this addiction to agriculture?—mechanization and an ill-developed logic of thought and action—the distinctive brand of synthetic thought characteristic of the Indian masses—mechanization as adoptable to the agricultural way of life.

INDIA, WHILE ROUGHLY only half the size of the United States, is inhabited by more than twice the population.

The total land area of India is 812 million acres; out of this surveyable area, land-use statistics are available for only 611 million acres, because the bulk of the remaining 201 million acres is covered by mountains, deserts and inaccessible forests. Out of the accessible 611 million acres, 266 million acres is the area sown, 58 million acres are currently fallow, 98 million acres are cultivable waste, 96 million acres are not available for cultivation, and 93 million acres are covered by forests.

TABLE 4 [1]

POPULATION AND LAND RESOURCES
IN INDIA, U.S.A. AND U.S.S.R.

(1)	(2)	(3)	(4)
	India	U.S.A.	U.S.S.R.
Population in millions	361	151	194
Land area in millions of acres	813	1905	5904
Area per capita in acres:			
All land	2.25	12.64	30.46
Agricultural area	.97	7.41	4.48
Arable land	.97	3.02	2.07

53

A farmer in the United States is a prosperous guy; hardy, stocky, sun-burnt and, maybe a small millionaire. His farm will be a few hundred acres in size with a cattle range, poultry house and a few other amenities that go with a farm house. His children go to school in the city; one or two of them may stay in the farm business. A symbol of peace and prosperity, the farm life produces nostalgic associations.

One has had a hard time disabusing the opinion of eager Americans who would go into raptures about the beauty of the farm life, far from the mad crowds. To them, it is hard to visualize the equivalent of "Ohio" as a by-word of eternal poverty and everlasting indebtedness.

Fragmentation of land holdings progressed with the passing of time. Generation after generation of children carved morsels from the grand old possession of the great grandfather. The rugged soil could tell of marriages which cost mortgages of sections; of plots that were sold to support children through school; of auctions that hawked big chunks of land to appease the ever-present vulture of family indebtedness. Eaten up successively by time and wants, the remnants which accrue to individual inheritors are generally too inadequate in size to provide sustenance to anybody.

The returns from the overworked land are a gamble on the monsoons. You wait for the rain. If it is a day earlier or later than planned, if its quantity is more or less than expected your whole crop for the year suffers or prospers. Usually, the poor peasant has to borrow to sow the field; he has to borrow to manure it; he has to borrow to survive in between sowing and harvesting, which period varies from six to eight months. And all the while he has to support a family consisting of his wife, four or five children and usually his aged parents. All this has to be done by means of the tiny little plot of land that has come to him through the ages.

In the face of these disheartening facts, of insistent mortgages and recurrent imperative demands, why does this old soul worry away at this barren spot, which is more a liability than an asset?

One of the basic elements in the insistence of the peasant is the fact that agriculture is not an *occupation* but a *way of life*. Underlying any question of why the peasant does not change his manner of cultivation or the scope of his work is the tacit assumption that agriculture is an occupation of his choice as a means of sustenance. If business is not good, quit it! It is so simple as that: what is the point in wasting time over beating a doubly dead horse? Can't he think, calculate, and quit?

He can think, and he does. He can calculate, and he does. He can quit but he does not.

Have you ever tried talking a poet into business, or an artist into a foremanship with Ford Motor Company? All the wealth, security, and prestige that the alternate occupation can offer will not do the trick. What is at stake is much more than money: it is one's very life. It is far beyond the liking of the job: one does not merely love his life. And so also to the Indian farmer, farming is his very life. Thru thick and thin, thru rain and shine, his farm is his life and he would not barter it for any promise, no matter how precious it might be.

So, when you talk of Indian agriculture, you are talking of the life of a people. The operation involves life and is therefore vital. And vital operations call for the best equipment and, more than that, perfect understanding.

Mechanical methods of cultivation would present themselves as the immediate logical step in improving the yield from the land.

However, even in the matter of introducing modern technical devices on the farm, which is but a first step towards mechanization, considerable non-cooperation on the part of the farmer has already been disclosed. Tractors lay rusting while crops keep dwindling. Does this mean that the farmer does not want to improve his lot? Or could there be some aspect of his thinking that has been overlooked and which may account for this behaviour?

When the attempt was made to teach a group of villagers through the medium of films, it was found that they had to be handled on a much lower level of co-ordinated understanding than was normal. For instance, if you were to teach them that the calf drinks milk from the udder of the cow, it must be done in a series of pictures—one in which the cow is shown, another the calf, a third one where the udder is prominent, a fourth showing the cow and the calf, and then a fifth one showing the cow in the actual process of milk feeding. If you were to show the last one alone, although their retina would register the sight, it would not produce any impression on the intellect, because it is not in a position to grasp the impression as a whole.

Applying this to agriculture, a demonstration of tractors might appear as a one-picture-piece. You create a visual impression on their minds. You tell them that this is the best way to do things. They nod "aye." But there it ends. What is missing in this chain between demonstration and reaction is that co-ordination which translates the nod into action. They do not go home and say to themselves: "That is something worth doing. It will cost me $24.23 to begin with, but over the years it will work out to be less than a penny a day. And the advantage I draw by way of higher yield will be at least $50.00 in the first year. So let me borrow the money and do it." The visual picture may remain unfaded, and so also the inspiring words of the instructor. But as Dickens described it:

> Sadly, sadly, the sun rose; it rose upon no sadder sight than the man of good abilities and good emotions, incapable of their directed exercise, incapable of his own help and his own happiness, sensible of the blight on him, and resigning himself to let it eat him away. [2]

Would this inadequate ability to co-ordinate present an

insurmountable barrier to improving agricultural pursuits in India?

No. It only means that reform has to be slow, sure and steady. No overnight jump from wooden plough to bulldozers may be expected; but there could certainly be a transition from wooden plough to iron plough. Maybe sometime later a small motor could be attached to the plough which would supply the power to cultivate the field. These two steps may well take at least two to three seasons. If the attempt is made to take a short-cut, that would be killing the goose that lays the golden egg: the goose of the farmer's adaptability which would lay the golden egg of improved farming and faster yields.

Perhaps the appropriate means of making mechanization acceptable to the masses are clearly illustrated in the popular acclaim of *Ambar Charka*. *Charka* is a spinning wheel. *Ambar* comes from the name of the inventor of the four-spindled charka, Ekambaranathan.

Ambar Charka is a hand-operated machine twenty-one inches long and high and sixteen inches across. Weighing twenty-six pounds, it costs $8.40. The hope is that the Ambar Charka will increase employment in the spinning and weaving trades. Estimates of how many more spinners will be employed run from 300,000 to 2,500,000. An Ambar Charka spinner can expect to earn about fifteen cents a day.

What makes the mechanical charka acceptable to the masses which cold-shoulder the tractor is the basic fact that in adopting the former, the peasant or village laborer feels that he is fulfilling his destiny more creatively. The charka is germane to his cherished aspirations: the single-spindle wheel was Gandhiji's revered symbol of the independence of the peasant in cloth production. The symbol was particularly powerful when India was obliged to export her cotton to Manchester and buy manufactured cloth back.

While the future of Ambar Charka is unknown, the charka's quick and definite appeal to the masses bespeaks the technique that ought to govern any approach to popularizing mechanization.

As to its politico-economic intonations:

> There is even more than the future of India's cloth workers tied up in the controversy over the Ambar Charka. The little machine with the whirring spindles is a symbol in its own way of the enormous problem India's planners face. That problem is to balance the drive for industrial expansion against the imperative need to make sure that the millions of people who live by village crafts are not wiped out by the big machine in the big factory.
>
> This is not a problem India has forgotten. In its second five-year plan, about $42,000,000, or more than 14 per cent of the industrial capital outlay, has been set aside for helping village and other small-scale industries. And the Prime Minister of India never tucks his daily rose into anything but a garment made of khadi—cloth woven and spun by hand. [3]

The mechanization of agriculture will be a far cry from the changes made to mechanical implements, such as the Ambar Charka, in industry. It is fraught with grave dangers if introduced immediately. The danger is due to the fact that changes in agriculture touch the vital cords of peasant existence in India. And, if a people, whose readiness to change is hampered by problems of co-ordinated action and understanding, are hustled to an entirely alien way of living, the result would be parallel to what happens when the clutch is released too soon in starting an automobile—a broken axle and complete cessation of all forward motion.

The foregoing should not be interpreted as a polite euphemism for the fact that the Indian peasant is just plain stupid. Far from it: illiteracy is never a by-word for ignorance. For instance, consider the results of the first election in the infant republic. The largest democratic electorate ever went to the polls to decide India's political future—a hundred and eighty million people, hardly eighteen per cent of whom could sign their names and who had never known how to question, but only to obey the almighty overlord on whose kingdom the sun never set; a people who suddenly knew that they were free and realized that they were hungry; a people on whom the organized machinery of the open propaganda of the Communist Party, which has undisputably the best co-ordinated activity in India, had been let loose for four full years of turmoil, trouble and tribulation. If suddenly the entire cadre of civil service were evacuated and an altogether new foreign diplomatic corps had to be built up; famine and pestilence ravaged the meagre means of subsistence of the people and an influx of immigrants was continually swamping the big cities, then the ruling party would certainly be at a disadvantage against an opposing political party which had none of the worries and all of the potentials for making political capital. Who would suspect that anything could be more tempting to a starving man than the bait of bread, and who could have dangled it more appealingly than the Communist Party of India? And they did.

Yet the election results revealed no dumb electorate; not one comprised of simple folks who could be beguiled by the precious promises of the "New Civilization." It must not be forgotten that the Government of India could not muster much by way of assets to place against the era of plenty and prosperity promised by the Communists—not during the first five years of independence when the mass of refugees and the pranks of nature conspired to aggravate the pangs of partition. History has borne out the fact that at this moment of trial, precisely when the hardest realities prompted the poor peasant to clutch at the straw of hope that the Communists so generously held out, his illiteracy did not find him altogether dumb. The Indian electorate exercised a wisdom that is easily equal to that of the most mature of electorates. The subtleties of the election results bear this out.

The Indian National Congress Party, which fought for India's independence, and which took the reins of administration in the first years of the country's independence, was given an overwhelming majority in the Central Legislature. Freedom to be bold enough to initiate new measures is admittedly essential to progress, particularly in a new nation. All the members of the Central Cabinet who stood for re-election were returned. In the industrial cities, the Communists were practically routed, the Congress being returned with a very decent majority.

However, the support given to the Congress Party was not unqualified. The people were not oblivious to the severe short-comings of some of its representatives. In most of the states, these particular persons who held cabinet positions prior to the elections were overthrown as a just tribute to the way in which they handled the trust reposed in them. Strict warnings were given by the electorate, particularly in Travancore-Cochin which leads the nation in literacy. With a bare majority the Congress Party had to maneuver a difficult coalition. Later in 1952, fresh elections had to be held, which showed that the Congress had not won back the confidence of the people, of Travancore-Cochin. In 1956, pending re-election, President's Rule had to be declared in the state because there was no party which had won adequate seats in the House of Representatives to form a government. In April 1957, the Communists won the general elections in the State of Kerala (the new state comprised of the native states of Travancore, Cochin and Malabar), and formed a government. In the summer of 1959, popular reaction against their earlier mandate was gathering momentum, and demonstrations against the Communist government were widespread. President's Rule was once again invoked.

Now, it stands to reason that a people who could exercise such fine refinements of political judgment in the very first attempt at deciding their own form of government, could not be quite dumb. If they could calculate, and give only 5.2 per cent of the seats to the Communists in the Central Legislature and 5.8 in the states, if they could give their support to enable formation of a strong central government and strong governments in strategic states, and yet record their protest against irresponsibile handling of popular confidence, they certainly are capable of refined judgment. They may be way off the mark of prudence in the cae of adopting profitable ways of agriculture. But this is not because they are dumb, but because their minds work in a way different from that which would facilitate prudent adoptions. A certain amount of analytical disposition is implied in the ability to make adjustments and take to new ways of electing. But the kind of reasoning that displays capabilities of subtle political judgment is more synthetic in nature. While the former evidences its skill in shredding situations to bits and splitting the narrowest hair, the latter excels in the art of immaculate judgment on issues from the widest perspective: combing the achievements or lack of them in the past and the trend of the present to peer into the promise of the future.

The fact that the Indian mind is synthetic has immediate relevance to the problem of mechanization of agriculture, for mechanization involves a new orientation and outlook. The resistance to machinery on the farm evidenced thus far is traceable, at least in part, to the fact that the suggestion has been made in the wrong form. Just as a born poet would feel unhappy rubbing shoulders with a crankshaft mechanic in an auto-factory, the poet—like Indian peasant finds himself at more than arm's length from suggestions which might disturb the tranquility and peace of his ancestral, though shrivelled, farm.

In order to make any effective appeal to the peasant, mechanization of agriculture will have to be presented to him as a process of synthetic reasoning. He has to be convinced not to adapt a few odd novelties, but to adopt certain amenities of life. In other words, machinery should become part of his life in some way similar to the almost organic relationship in which his bullocks stand to him.

Suggestions of "making a fast buck" would not be the best means, because wealth is *not* the standard of social status. Certainly money is welcome and desired as a means of transactions, but it is far from being a measuring rod for prestige. The *nouveau riche* is under the spell of silent ostracization. Hence, the use of machinery on the farm or, worse than that, a mechanized way of life, presented as a short cut to money making will be far from welcome.

A group adoption of this new way of life will be practical for two primary reasons. For one thing, it somewhat reduces the stigma of ostracization when sinning is done in good company. For another, a certain degree of collectivization of land will be necessary for effective use of heavy machinery.

The millions of refugees, uprooted from their home and hearth, may be a possible "control" group. When they are rehabilitated on an adequately large area, they have to be provided with homes and occupations. In one of the areas which have been reclaimed, if a refugee colony were started, and if they then were given the means to mechanize agriculture, it might well be an easier process than revolutionizing the sedate patterns of life in a long-established village. The refugees, in their keenness for settlement, would probably be less prejudiced toward mechanization than an established village. And a new beginning could be a better one.

The Community Projects which are in operation in many parts of India today are helpful starting points for slowly inviting and inducing the peasant to modify his way of life with the aid of machinery. Here again, the recreational facilities enjoyed in common, such as the mass TV programs for groups of villages, mentioned in Chapter Four, could be helpful means for sponsoring collective activity. The recurrent acts of common recreation would contribute substantially to a common endeavour at adopting a new way of life altogether. The machinery should positively be presented to the peasant as only a *means* to a better living. Many of the unspoken fears of the peasant today pertain to the feeling that these machines, once let in, would start demanding despotic attention and care. And a poet would rather be without the mechanical device than sacrifice all his peace and comfort for the sake of an inanimate gadget. Show the peasant that it is a way of life of his own choosing. Without breaking his wooden image of the plough, and his animal image of the bullock, invite him to a better way of *life, not* a mere increase of luxuries.

CHAPTER SIX

DIVIDED WE FALL

Symbol and substance—previous land consolidation efforts—
the absent zemindar and the cultivating peasant—need for
designing experiments incorporating human variables—operation consolidation: (1) legislation (2) *Bhoodan Yajna* (3)
impact of Western ideas—the incestous tie to the soil—kite-
flying in a new context.

SOMERSET MAUGHAM WROTE the story "The Kite." It is about
a family of kite-flyers to whom the prime concern in life was
the kite. The son, Herbert, got his first kite for Christmas when
he was a boy; and as years went by he flew bigger and better
kites with his father and mother. When Herbert was engaged
to be married to Betty, he could no longer go kite-flying on
Saturday afternoons with his mother. But Herbert expected
Betty to come around to flying the kite soon after their marriage. However, the idea of a grown man flying a kite was con-
temptible to Betty. Herbert's doting on the kite cut Betty
deeply and she protested, only to have Herbert walk out on
her to his kite. Outraged, Betty smashed the kite when Herbert was at his parents'; and Herbert took revenge by refusing
to pay a penny to Betty in alimony. On Betty's complaint,
Herbert was brought before the magistrate and was asked why
he did not obey the court order to pay alimony. "I said I

wouldn't pay her and I won't, not after she smashed my kite. And if you send me to prison, I'll go to prison."[1] Herbert didn't pay, and was sent to prison.

The innumerable small peasants who plod their weary way to, through, and from the tiny holdings of theirs are flying a kite of their own. It is a very small kite, but entirely satisfactory. Herbert's infatuation with kite-flying may seem infantile: so will be the obstinate devotion with which the peasant holds on to his small piece of land. It is not surprising that even as Betty could not see what there was in kite-flying, the peasant's phantasy concerning his plot will strike the outsider as, at best, irrational. If the peasant were to be teased about his sub-subsistence struggle, he could be expected to retort that not only did he fly the kite ever since he was a kid, but that his father and his grandfather also flew the kite of cultivating the same tiny piece of earth. Any condescending allowance for his indulgence—"If you want to fly your silly old kite, you fly it"— would grate with his entire outlook. The reason is that even more than Herbert doted on his kite, the peasant dotes on the microscopic plot of land that comes to him from the ages gone by, bequeathed by revered ancestors. And if any Betty of modernization were unceremoniously to break up the kite of the Indian peasant's holdings in order to consolidate land, such a move would be refused even a single penny of the alimony of cooperation: the peasant would prefer to go to the prison of poverty than pay for the upkeep of his land as a part of an alarmingly huge farm.

> It may be that in some dim, confused way it represents an ideal of freedom and adventure. And you know, when a man once gets bitten by the virus of the ideal not all the King's doctors and not all the King's surgeons can rid him of it.[2]

If the precious and poor possession represents an ideal to the peasant, the surest means of consolidating landholdings to enable mechanization of agriculture would be close and rigorous study of the nature and extent of this idealism. To this end, certain basic facts will be helpful.

The consolidation of land-holdings has long been discussed as a theoretical measure for bettering Indian agriculture. Before Partition, the Punjab was one spot where the effort had met with relatively more success than other parts of the country. In one instance, as many as *two hundred* holdings had to be consolidated to form *one acre* of land! This will give an idea of the extensive fragmentation of land holdings which has resulted in the course of history.

In a democracy, any inroad into personal property has to be on the basis of personal consent. The Punjab experiments were based on consent of the majority. If the majority of farmers in an area were for consolidation, the holdings were consolidated irrespective of the non-consent of the minority. The experiment has not been a thundering success.

It would appear that it is not merely a question of prudent preference for a profitable system of operation that is involved in the question of consolidating land holdings. It may not be extremely difficult to demonstrate to the farmer that his labors would be better rewarded if they could be applied on a wider scale and over a wider area. The opposition to a merger of land holdings, similar in nature to a consolidation of small businesses in order to create a more powerful single body, may seem oddly strange. The problem posed by the mental difficulties of the peasant in grasping the point of any persuasive demonstration of consolidated cultivation, has been indicated earlier. Attention may therefore be focused on another pertinent issue.

To the farmer, whose ancestry as well as posterity are inextricably interwoven with that small plot of farmed-out and therefore agriculturally useless land, it represents more than what the kite did to Herbert in the Maugham story. To the farmer, the loss of that bit of land is tantamount to the end-all of his earthly existence. Losing his individuality in a merger with a hundred others cannot, therefore, be very pleasing to the peasant.

And, the Constitution of the Republic of India guarantees the Fundamental Right to Private Property. This applies to the tiniest land holding as well as to the largest. The recognition of the inalienable right of property is seen in the *Zemindari* Abolition.

The *Zemindari* system of land tenure dates back to the days of Lord Cornwallis who was the Governor-General of India in the late 1790's. This was a convenient device which simultaneously ensured the collection of revenue for the Government, while at the same time freeing it from the bother of collecting same. Similar in principle to the Feudal System of England, where land belonging to the King was divided among his nobles who paid rental for the privilege, under the Indian *Zemindari* system of land tenure, the land was distributed to the highest bidders of revenue. They in turn sublet the use of the land to people who promised the highest rental. The latter were frequently squeezed according to the whims and fancies of the landlord to cater to his needs. Care of the land was not among their worries. Theirs was not to worry how to improve the land but only how to sublet—and collect. The government was pleased as long as it did not have to worry about a steady revenue which could be increased as the needs of the State mounted.

Huge holdings of this type are a rarity today. Under *Zemindari* tenure, huge chunks of land lay wasting under the patronage of the big landlord (*Zemin*) who would be absent from the scene (Absentee Landlordism) except when the rents were due. As a consequence of the apathy of the owner, the land which was cultivated would be overworked and undernourished, the tenant not having the resources to replenish the land himself. Thus, on the one side is obtained insignificant fragments of land under the corroding influence of repeated partition among successive generations of small peasants, and on the other, bulk holdings which lay languishing under apathic ownership and poor tenancy.

Whatever be the appropriate size of collective farms, it is essential that the farmer enjoy the privilege of providing his own individual touches to the work of art which his vocation represents to him. This would entail experiments in a new dimension altogether.

The design of the experiments currently in vogue usually has a "control" group against which the productivity or lack of productivity of a particular method of cultivation is tested. In this case, where the human factor is involved, the separation of the elements of "pure" individual initiative from such initiative displayed under conditions of consolidated land holdings makes objective assessment far more difficult than usual. The experiment has to reckon with psychological as well as biochemical factors; on the one hand, there is the whole range of individual ability which can adapt itself to changing circumstances, and on the other, is the probably more easily controllable factor of biochemical variation of the soil. Most of the agricultural experiments have confined themselves to observing the changes in the latter alone. For instance, when the productivity of a new method of manuring is tested, one plot of land is cultivated without any manure, another with manure A and a third with manure B. Assuming that other conditions, such as fertility, natural factors, i.e., sunshine, rain, etc. are fairly uniform over all the three plots of land, comparison is then made of the yield of the three plots.

With the introduction of the human factor, the problem is not merely dimensionally increased by one, but it becomes an altogether new *conceptual* problem. Modern statistical methods will have to modify their tools in order to cope with this new kind of problem. Whether it will result in the invention of an altogether new technique of analysis, as in economics with The Theory of Games, or not, is too early to say. However, it may be noted in passing that the interaction between the individual and the form of land holding is likely to assume a dimension which might easily defy control. For instance, there might be irrational methods, i.e., those methods which are not completely open to analysis in terms of visible phenomena. Farmer A might be invoking the Spirits that Farmer B cannot. Suffice it to say at this point, that the socio-statistical experiments to decide the nature and extent of collective ownership and farming of land in India call for extremely complicated designing.

Associated with the forms of proprietorship are the memories that India has of other experiments of similar nature. Examples are not hard to find. The form of land ownership in China under the communists has certainly instilled some undefined fears in the Indian peasant. While he does not know for sure as to what is taking place there (who does?) the mass movement involved in the transition has served to caution him of any move in the direction of vesting the ownership of his land in any hands other than his own. This is quite likely to prove to be one of those intangible and fairly unassailable oppositions to any suggestions of mass methods of cultivation.

Whether or not the large estates should be broken into small ones is, from this point, a debatable issue. If the new methods of farming would call for consolidation on a large scale, the breaking up of the large estates would be unwise, for, in addition to the wastage involved in parcelling up land (which is considerable, inasmuch as the area taken up by the boundaries alone amounts to five per cent of the cultivable area), it would give rise to the personal involvement verging on infatuation.

However, the large percentage of the land under cultivation has already been fragmented. Hence the problem of piecing it together in some form or other is indispensable to implement the reforms through the introduction of machinery.

Legislative enactment would have to battle with the bitter

clauses of Fundamental Rights in the Constitution if consolidation were to be forced by the law. Since there is almost no indication of any desire or design on the part of the present Government to ride rough-shod over the intimate and inalienable rights of the people, this possibility is only theoretical, or at least very distant in the present context.

Co-operation is the last hope of the Indian peasant; if co-operation fails, the last hope of the Indian peasant fails. Much water has flowed under the bridge since this statement in the early 1900's. National emancipation has rendered the act of co-operation much more meaningful and respectable than it was under the patronizing surveillance of a kind of quasi-paternalism wherein the high and lofty official weight of the British officers was used to bring about consent to and consolidation of small land-holdings. With the dawn of independence, the common endeavors of the villagers achieved a better glow of spontaneity; but it would be bold indeed to read in this the immediate consummation of the goal of co-operation as far as land-holdings being merged into bigger units is concerned.

The mystic land of India appears to defy many of the usual means of bringing about a change in the size of agricultural holdings in order to make them amenable to the advantages of modern machinery. Demonstrations of prudent advantages seem to fall flat. Legislative enforcement involves drastic inroads into the rights to private property. Co-operative consolidation from the popular level seems so far and remote. Is there a way out?

Acharya Vinoba Bhave's *Bhoodan Yajna* seems to provide the answer.

Acharya (Teacher) Vinoba Bhave, easily one of the most devoted among the living disciples of Mahatma Gandhi, set out on foot, on a Mission of Land Offering in April, 1951. *Yajna* means sacrifice or sacrificial offering; *Bhoo* means the earth. Just as the name indicates, he set out *not* to *get* land but to encourage the *sacrificial offering* of land. He started by asking the rich of the villages to give part of their land to the needy among them, to those who did not have any land. Treking from village to village, this frail little man is perhaps closest to the heart of rural India. His mission is to "loot with affection." And amazingly enough, his looting is catching up as village after village offers its land to him for redistribution.

A total of over 2 1/2 million acres of land has been conveyed to Acharya for redistribution. His goal is to collect fifty million acres, nearly one-fifth of India's cultivated acreage.

The symbolic value of the movement is indeed very high. This revolutionary method has brought to light the responsiveness of the villager to suggestions of sacrifice. When it is remembered that it is the self-same landowners who oppose land reform legislation and who do not promote co-operative endeavors on rural levels, who willingly bow to the begging—and demanding—Acharya, it definitely offers a clear indication of an important element in any attempt at effective reorganization of land-holdings. It would bear repetition to say that the peasant would respond to the call to make a sacrifice for better fulfillment of his destiny more readily than if he were to be forced by law or by lawlessness.

"My aim," says Acharya, "is to bring about a three-fold revolution. Firstly, I want a change in people's hearts; secondly, I want to create a change in their lives; and thirdly, I want to change the social-structure."

Changing the social-structure calls for change from within. While Acharya's revolutionary redistribution process is a strong catalytic agent, the chemical reaction between the masses and new ideas itself will have to be a continuous process. "The old order changeth, yielding place to new" only grudgingly. To the old men who are still at the helm of rural affairs, new ways of cultivation are an anathema. The time and effort expended on teaching the older generation new tricks, "over their dead bodies" so to speak, may be used with greater advantage to present the challenge of modernization to the young. If the young are acquainted with progressive ideas of farming methods, there would be the possibility of their influencing farming methods.

The considerable interest that the 4-H groups in the United States have been evidencing in Indian agriculture is certainly commendable. One of the activities sponsored by the 4-H is the exchange of delegates. The visiting team from India spends their six-month stay in the States with two or three different farmers, observing the practical application of machinery to farming operations. In the evenings, the members of the team meet with the local 4-H groups, exchanging ideas on farming.

Perhaps more important than the actual mechanical applications themselves, is the *spirit of adventure and adaptation* among the younger generation in the United States from which the visitors would benefit greatly. Yet, being so obvious, this stands in danger of being overlooked or taken for granted. Taking it for granted might very well leave the visitors in a worse state than before their encounter with the enterprising nation: "They are a smart lot: they work hard; and they have all the means which they use properly. Poor us! What do we have?"

A corrective to this quite possible reaction is an imperative necessity in order to channelize the useful impact of Western Ways. While merely recalling the wonderful things that the delegates saw, heard, and did, by themselves could be more disheartening (i.e., by their unattainable splendor), if the young potential agriculturists themselves are trained to act in groups, it would serve to transmit the impact of personal experience to the clogging wheels of despondency.

The prejudices of the younger generation are less hard than those of the older generation, but the former will be more sensitive to interference with personal status than the latter. This would mean that while there may be better chances of the younger generation's being induced to be co-operative in cultivation, they would not stand any suggestions of being nose-led by other people.

Perhaps a happy compromise between the move to preserve the indigenous nature of initiative unsullied by outside interference and the profusion of outside guidance now existing, is seen in the Ecumenical Work Camps held under the auspices of the World Council of Churches.

In the Ecumenical Work Camps, a group of people who want to build a new community come together to plan ahead in detail the kind of houses they want to build, the schools, the place of worship, etc. that they want to have in their community. The Work Camps enable the groups to come together as many times as necessary. By the time the group is ready to start building, they would have exchanged and expressed their ideas in the group so many times that they would be prepared to work together. And they very carefully supervise the building of houses and other buildings to ensure efficiency and minimum cost. When they finally start living together, they are so personally involved that the community life enjoys a spontaneous vim and vigor which is quite a quality of its own.

The delegates who visit the U.S. under the 4-H schemes could probably "sell" the community project idea, particularly to the younger generation. They may be able to devise profitable methods of organization and demonstration suited to the local levels so that consolidation will be a very natural outcome of the co-ordinated desire for individual emancipation, in an atmosphere of sacrificial undertaking for the better fulfillment of one's vocation in life.

This fulfillment is likely to remain skin-deep so long as a deep-seated perversion in the peasant's relationship with the land is not rectified. This perversion is what may be termed the incestuous tie to the soil.

Erich Fromm discusses the religions of the world through history and discloses a shifting of emphasis from a purely patriarchal to a blending between matriarchal and patriarchal elements. In the relationship to mother, there is little the child can do to regulate or control. The relationship to the father, on the other hand, can be controlled. It can be easily established that India has had a culture of a matriarchal structure. The innumerable and significant Indian goddesses, Kali, Saraswathi, Parvathi, Bhoodevi (goddess Earth) for instance, illustrate this structure.

As a result of the matriarchal structure, there can be found a number of examples of the matriarchal kind of relatedness to mother, blood and soil, even where the social forms are not matriarchal any more. To quote Fromm:

> The positive aspect (of attachment to the mother figure) is a sense of affirmation of life, freedom and equality which pervades the matriarchal structure . . . The negative aspect: by being bound to nature, to blood and soil, man is blocked from developing his individuality and his reason. [3]

Relatedness to the mother figure can turn into a state of fixation. Associated with fixation to mother is the effort to procure motherly love in a neurotic, magical way. The magic idea is: if I make myself into a helpless child, mother (Mother Earth) is bound to appear (in the form of bountiful crops) and take care of me.

On the other hand, mastery over nature (as is manifested in industrial production, etc.) is a positive aspect of patriarchal structure. Instead of remaining a child and incapable of progress, man forces himself to develop his reason, to build up a man-made world of ideas, principles and man-made things which replace nature as a ground of existence and security.

When man is forced to develop his reason, and assert himself, he would naturally be fulfilling himself as a human being. Man becomes *human* to the extent that he rises above the animal level of existence which is one of perfect harmony with nature, depending on Mother Earth to feed him, contented with what she gives him, venturing not to struggle for more lest he displease his mother. The security that he enjoys must now be bartered in the name of freedom for this world of man-made things. Modernization beckons him to the adventure of ideas, but the security that he had known, that his father and grandfather and great-grandfather had known and cherished, invites him to stay on the pathway of *status quo*. The advantages of tractors and bulldozers are, to him, promises yet to be proven; while the submarginal subsistence that he has been accustomed to through the ages is something that he can count on. The exercise of his freedom makes him feel that he stands on the edge of a steep precipice—he may climb up or fall down.

The mental attitude of the Indian peasant is strongly characterized by this hovering between the dead yesterday and the unborn morrow, unwilling to be born. In the twilight, the shades of uncertainty hovering around the unborn morrow of mechanization assume alarming proportions and draw weird figures. Startled, the peasant runs back to his Mother Earth, choosing the security of the womb to the possibility of postnatal effort.

This hesitancy is neither unique nor novel. The Old Testament tells the story of a group of people who had an incestuous tie to the land in which they lived. In Fromm's words:

> *Human History* is described as beginning with the expulsion of man from paradise, from the soil in which he was rooted, and with which he felt one. *Jewish* history is described as beginning with the command to Abraham to leave the country in which he was born, and to go "to a country which thou knowest not." From Palestine, the tribe wanders to Egypt; from there, again it returns to Palestine. But the new settlement is not final either. The teachings of the prophets are directed against the new incestuous involvement with the soil and nature as it was manifest in Canaanitic idolatory.

They proclaimed the principle that a people who has re-
gressed from the principles of reason and justice to those
of the incestuous tie to the soil, will be driven away from
its soil and will wander in the world homeless until it has
fully developed the principles of reason, until it has overcome
the incestuous tie to the soil and nature; only then can the
people return to their homeland, only then will the soil be a
blessing, a *human* home freed from the curse of incest. The
concept of the Messianic time is that of the complete victory
over the incestuous ties, and the full establishment of the
spiritual reality of moral and intellectual conscience, not
only among the Jews, but among all peoples of the earth. [4]

The question that arises is: what shall correspond to the
"wandering in the world, homeless" in the life of the Indian
peasant? Should he be dispossessed of his land and hold it in
common with the others—perhaps under a system of collective
farming? Or should he be driven to work in factories in urban
areas, feel disgusted, and return as a repentant prodigal, to
the land which he forfeited because of his incestuous tie?

Considered strictly from the point of view of humanistic
psychoanalysis, the *Bhoodan Yajna* (sacrificial land gift),
smacks of perpetuation of the incestuous tie to the soil. Acharya
Vinoba Bhave was greeted in the different villages with the
cry: "The God who gives land is come!" This welcome to
the Eternal Donor of good things is quite in keeping with the
philosophy of the peasant whose sacred writings assure him
that God interferes in human history by direct intervention in
the form of one or the other incarnations. In the welcome cry
the magical idea is clearly discernible—when I make myself
helpless like a child, Mother will appear and give me land.

An exceedingly complicated interplay of attitudes (of a
sense of affirmation of life on the positive side, and the passive
dependent role of an eternal receiver, uninterested in striking
out on one's own, on the negative side) makes prognosis a
veritable Gordian knot. But then, it is one of life's perplexing

rainbows, made out of threatening rain and promising sunlight. The threatening rain of perpetual incestuous tie to the soil is intercepted by the promising sunlight of the potentials of a living faith. Even as the certainty of Mother's affection makes the children strong and confident, the Indian peasant's dependence on winds and rain, sun and soil, if healthy, can be a strong bulwark in personal and national life. This strength would leave both the individuals and the nation unruffled when tossed by the tides of time.

But this faith is yet to be shaped. Today there are only the potentials of such a vibrant faith.

These potentials peep out from beneath a pervasive fatalism. In the form of fatalism these potentials are like the waterfall dashing against hills and corroding the land around: their effect is watched with uncertain concern. When transformed into living faith, the same potentials are like the waterfall harnessed to generate power and irrigate barren lands: their wholesome effect is a dependable bedrock of personal and national life.

The supplanting of fatalism by faith is a time-consuming process. However, in the Indian context, this seems to be a *must*.

In the long run, the transformance of the fear of uncertainty into the faith of tranquility must address itself to the question of "wandering homeless," a necessary interim state of affairs.

To this end, in terms of Herbert's infatuation of kite-flying three alternatives seem open: (1), Herbert to court prison and Betty to live in separation; (2), Betty to take to kite-flying and go kite-flying with Herbert; (3), Betty to co-operate with Herbert and go kite-flying in the immediate, but to work with a competent psychiatrist to transform the symbolic security of Herbert's mother's kite into a significant source of inspiration for Herbert to become *human*.

In terms of the peasant and the land, these alternatives

would suggest: (1), perpetuation of the incestuous tie, mechanization ending where the peasant's holdings begin; (2), encouragement of the incestuous tie, passing on some small machinery on the sly; (3), simultaneous effort to bring about equitable redistribution of the land, and the weaning of the peasant from his undue fixation to the land by demonstrating mechanization of agriculture to be a creative manner of fulfilling his own destiny.

The prophets of the glory that was India in the days before the advent of machines could be involuntary accessories to the first alternative. Green grass, yellowing rice, ripening mangoes—all can create nostalgia; but preoccupation with them generally tends to slur over the dirty squalor of present life with its under-nourished and disease-ridden bodies, and the sapping of vitality in general that worms its way through the greenery because the greenery itself goes pale from insufficient replenishment of the soil.

Another involuntary accessory to the perpetuation of the incestuous tie of the peasant to the soil is the advocate of land reform by itself. If the land-hungry peasant is given a plot of land to cultivate and it is hoped that he would use all the advantages of modern machinery and methods of cultivation, a spectacle is likely to be witnessed similar to that of a swan which no sooner got out of the water than it found itself almost involuntarily being drawn into the water again. Land by itself would not bring the peasant's powers of reason and his self-emancipatory urge to the fore: on the other hand, the posession of land may induce in him a false sense of security which would lull him to complacency. In 1950, India declared war on the food front; but the slogan hardly made any dent on the various battlefronts of rural fields. The incestuous tie presented a hard core of conservatism. Without a concerted effort to cure the villager of his incestuous tie, even the scattering of tractors in the villages will only be ineffective in improving the villager's lot.

In his remarkable speech at Harvard, Adlai E. Stevenson said:

> Armed with a fanatical faith
> and a program of *dogmatic reform*
> in a time of tension and change,
> already disposing of vast armies
> and master of a third of the world,
> forever seeking new strength and new support
> in the troubled awakening of the great new continents,
> it is a force we can underestimate only at the risk of
> our own destruction. [5]

(verse form supplied for the purpose of emphasizing the component thoughts)

The "it" is international communism.

Dogmatic reform is the particular component that pertains to the present discussion of Indian agricultural reform via the third alternative, viz., a *simulataneous effort* to bring about equitable redistribution of the land, and the weaning of the peasant from his undue fixation to the land by demonstrating mechanization of agriculture to be a creative means of fulfilling his own destiny.

Dogmatic reform has made its dramatic bid to the loyalty and support of the masses in a thousand villages in Telengana District in Andhra State, and in Vyalaar in Alleppy and Cherthalai districts in Travancore, now part of Kerala State. Both reform movements set out to redistribute land among the masses by forcefully taking possession of the land and repudiating tenancy obligations; both movements were forcefully put down.

Even if the redistribution were effected, it would not have achieved any lasting benefit to the soil or the peasant for the simple reason that (matriarchal) possession of land would not by itself usher (patriarchal) elements of initiative and self-emancipatory urges to the fore. What is needed is the weaning of the peasant from his undue fixation to the land. Redistribution of land to the tiller is like Betty's co-operating with Herbert to go kite-flying. In psychiatric terms, this is the stage where a transference is developed in the patient who sees the psychiatrist as the mother or father, wife or husband, sister or brother whom the patient craves for.

Even if the Communists were to effect land redistribution, it would only be this stage of transference. It is a powerful stage which contains both promise and portent. Should the psychiatrist succeed in counter-transference, in which the patient is gradually able to understand himself as the psychiatrist understands him and his problems, the patient will have a good chance of full recovery. But the process is neither easy nor standard. Even so, winning the following of the masses by working them up to the stage of transference, by providing the image of a benevolent donor of land and defender of rights, is relatively an easy one. But that of effecting a counter-transference, of weaning the peasant from his fixation on land to developing his own reasoning powers and determination to take an active role in shaping his life, is an arduous task that calls for conviction, courage and strenuous work.

Apparently, the imagination of the youth has not yet been appropriately fired by the potency of this challenge. Village work remains, by and large, a dull, colorless endeavor, fit to be the last refuge of an educated unemployed. It is small wonder that Chester Bowles raises "some fundamental questions" based on his impressions of a personal visit to a number of Community Development Projects, which sprung from an Indo-American Technical Cooperation Plan two years before in 1953, during his term of office as United States Ambassador to India.

Last but not least what about India's greatest natural resources—her young people? Today many thousands of students in India are frustrated and insecure. How rapidly and

fully can these potentially explosive intellectuals be tied into
the dynamic growth of India? [6]

The antedote to the "Dogmatic reform" platform of the
Communists, the means of bringing lasting health and happiness to rural India, and the harnassing of "potentially explosive
intellectuals" to the dynamic growth of India, all call for a
philosophy of action which rises above the mere mechanics
of hobnobbing with village life. Only the vision that can command a broader sweep than that of the immediate land reform,
and foresee the direction of current activity, can survive the
outburst of uncertain enthusiasm. If the Communists take up
arms to cut up the land ahead of the legislative procedures
of the Government, it is not mortal. If the industrial workers
are led out on strikes every now and then, it is grave, but again
not mortal. But if creative foresight does not plan for the reha-
bilitation of the peasant as a psychic self, if the process of
counter-transference is not thought about and planned for
simultaneously with that of the transference stage, then it is
mortal. Where there is no vision, the people perish and the
plans perish. The tides of time will carry down in their swift
movement, the drifting, the uncertain, and the visionless; and
history will stink with the corpses of the youth of India, killed
in the unfought battle of ideas, surrendered to the forces of
commitment without reflection—unless the deeper yearnings of
the masses are understood and their matriarchal seeking of
security carefully supplanted by patriarchal affirmation of
initiative.

This bid to supplant will necessarily have to grapple with
more unseen than seen forces. Added to the ordinary reason
that the conscious mind is only a small fragment of the unconscious mind is the additional reason that symbolism has a pervasive place in Indian life. A brief discussion of the same will
be undertaken subsequently. Such discussions, while uncover-
ing the labyrinth of opposing attitudes, may also give a clue

to the underlying basic factors of anxiety and insecurity which attempt to gain expression in the forgotten language of dreams and seemingly irrational actions. In the meantime, divided we fall. Divided into a million minute plots of land, each with a small marginal ridge around it, the less than half the area of India which is available for cultivation is further reduced; and the small size prevents any effective actions for improving the yield.

So divided, the submarginal farms are an open invitation to any demagogue who can conveniently make opportunist capital out of the farmers' desperate search for security in land-holdings. Small land-holdings, if swayed by small thinking, are bound to culminate in crises common to any process of psychiatric transference stopped before countertransference. This halfway house between present poverty and future prosperity, if built by dogmatic reform, can be the worst opiate of the people. In order to combat that opiate, enable an active peasant life reform to be carried on, and to enlist the support of the young intellectuals—a philosophy of action has to be evolved. This philosophy of action must recognize the basic planks of the old order: the family basis of life and the relationship between the older and the younger generations.

THE FAMILY PLANK OF A
PHILOSOPHY OF ACTION

So-and-so of such-and-such family—traditional structure of
Hindu society and changes of the same—influence of the
family on young people away from home—marriage, a family
matter—differing past orientations call for different approaches—dangerous demolition of traditional images—wisdom of the old and wit of the young.

SOONER OR LATER, the zealous reformer will bounce against the
intangible, but rather inflexible, boundaries of the age-long
structure of Indian life.

It might come abruptly as a dramatic "no" to the soaring
schemes of rural upliftment, or as a sudden withdrawal of the
young men who had been so co-operative in the programs of
action that were being so beautifully unfolded.

Or it may be unostentatious. The villagers will continue to
be very polite in the traditional manner; the children may still
come to the centers of community activity: and even the young
men may continue to be present at the programs. But then
will begin a general slackening of enthusiasm, a slight drop in
attendance, a milder tone in their choruses of "yea." And before you can say "Jack Robinson," all that you have built up
in that community is gone with the wind.

This *volte-face* can be ruinous. It may suggest that community development efforts are being erected upon sandy foundations. Perhaps with deeper digging hard bedrock may be discovered. This digging is therefore worth trying.

It is said that the most frequently used word in English language is the monosyllable "I." If a similar count were possible in the common language of India (which does not exist) it is quite likely to be "we." Individuals just do not exist in Indian society. This does not mean that there is no place for the individual: there most certainly is. But he is not the *unit* of social structure. With all his glory, with all the respect that might be due him, he is still so-and-so of *such-and-such family*. The people do not count you as a separate entity, because you never were nor are a separate entity, from birth till death.

The family, as the primary unit of the organization of social life, occupies a very unique place; unique, because the family in India is quite different from the famly in the United States or in Great Britain or in China. The individualist element in American family life is now cutting into the traditional structure of British family life and into the community basis of Chinese family organization. But the old oak of the Indian family weathers all storms as it has done through the ages, still securely nestling under its spreading branches all its siblings whether they be far or near, in spite of the invasions of different armies or the inroads into the patterns of family life by outside societies.

This old oak was significantly assailed by the Second World War. The catastrophe shook the foundations of the family way of Indian life; but the family emerged, strengthened in its deep foundations even if shorn of weaker elements. How this came about would be an instructive inquiry.

The Hindu way of life compartmentalizes society into four main watertight sections: the *Brahmin* (priestly class), the *Kshatriya* (ruling class), the *Vaisya* (artisan and merchant class) and the *Sudra* (working class). These main "castes" are those into which you are born, and, just as you can neither influence nor change your birth, are unalterable. The members of the artisan class enjoy the services of the working class over the generations, the farmer father being served by the worker father, the farmer son by the worker son and so on down the line. Defense of the realm was an indispensable necessity in the early days of human history when man lived in clusters of small communities, and any intelligent social organization calls for someone to take care of defense. This was the duty of the *Kshatriya* caste. When production, trade and defense were taken care of, someone could sit down to study and do research: the *Brahmins.*

This sensible system of economic ordering had the blessing of the religious order. The worker who was bound to the land was to consider his servitude a privilege; he certainly was destined to fare better in the next life, in proportion to his services to the earthly masters. Services to the *Brahmin* were almost the highest sacred duty that any one could perform. The *Kshatriya* held power and had pomp: he also sought the blessings of the *Brahmin.* And the *Vaisya* was the backbone of the society: his vocation was hallowed through its homage to Mother Earth.

The Caste System has worked out a careful method of compensation. The *Brahmin,* who is most respected, has neither money nor power. Like the Levite in the Old Testament, he has to live on whatever support the community gives him; and the community has a moral obligation to take good care of the one who looks after its soul. The *Kshatriya* has power and riches which would be good enough compensation to keep him on duty as the defender of the realm, as well as to induce him to keep on his head the crown under which lay all uneasiness in the days of monarchy. The merchant and the farmer enjoy the security of a peaceful home; and the worker gets his wages in kind, not merely for the duration of the agricultural operations but also over the year at different festival seasons. Thus everybody is taken care of, and enjoys a sense of integral usefulness to the community.

Learning was the monopoly of the *Brahmin* who alone

could interpret the Scriptures. The other three castes had little to do with studies: in fact, the workers were prohibited from learning how to read and write. With the advent of the British in the 1600's, schools were set up for the underprivileged (who incidentally were apparently more amenable to proselytization). Some of the more enlightened native states, (the total number of native states at the time of the Independence of India was over 600) took the cue and made education available to the low-caste Hindu as well. When they started to learn, they realized that there could be more to life than mere survival. The rapid growth of industries made it possible to think in terms of gainful employment in a system which did not go by the color of one's skin, but by ability for hard work. The giant was awakening.

Foreign travel was another taboo under the old order. It took years of pioneering and daring before the force of religious ostracization could be mellowed in its onslaught. Slowly but steadily, people did begin to move out to see the rest of the world. The travellers brought back with them not only news but also views of different ways of life.

The Second World War offered opportunities of world-wide travel to a number of young and ready men who were prepared to break through barriers of caste if only they could, by so doing, better their levels of existence. Defense services offered war time employment. The recruits into the army, navy and air services could not only live better but also travel widely. And they came back to a country whose face and fortune were undergoing rapid transformation. Back home, they were up against the very problems of life from which they sought temporary refuge in the war. Their tremendous energies could be harnessed for better or worse. In any case, once having discovered the delight of foreign travel, they were not going to be tied down to the old home and hearth.

Thanks to a fairly irresponsible system of education, almost totally irrelevant to life, as well as an inadequately planned process of industrialization, travel offered almost the only means of supplementing the diminishing returns of land. "Young men, go East or West—to Calcutta or Bombay." Calcutta, for instance, is a refuge of many ambitious young men. Soon after completing high school, they learn stenography and short-hand and go to the biggest city. There they have to face keen local competition and try to secure some back-breaking secretarial job. After the usual office hours, 9 A.M. to 5 P.M., with half-an-hour or an hour of lunch break, some of them put themselves through school from 6 P.M. to 9 P.M., in an attempt to finish their formal education.

All the big cities are continuously over-crowded with these "student-refugees" if one may so designate them. This migratory population is usually composed of men in the late teens and early twenties. Some of the older ones might have gone to different parts of the world during the war, some may be leaving home for the first time; but all of them are anxious to travel and not be bound to their own small villages.

How has the traditional structure of family and social life sustained this iconoclastic tendency in the wake of the war and of the independence of the nation?

Admittedly, the youth enjoys the freedom from the immediate supervision of the home when they go to cities hundreds of miles away from their village. They breathe a new sense of responsibility and enjoy its power. They enjoy something which is best appreciated only when it is recalled that post-natal care by parents usually persists through marriage. This contributes to the continued dependency of the young men. Even after marriage, they do not necessarily live away from the family of origin, which makes dependence on home a continuous phenomenon. Therefore, the freedom that the "student refugees" enjoy assumes greater significance. The ability to earn on their own makes them independent of the family; and in a certain measure, the parents in their old age become dependent on them. It is a tribute to the solidarity of Indian family structure that these young men, with all their independence, still share their small pay checks with the folks at home and consult them on important matters.

It is more or less clear that this continuing relationship is not accidental. It seems to imply that the home is still sweet home.

Distilling through differing layers of avocation and circumstances, this sweetness of home takes varying shades, but the essence of the fragrance emitted is the same all over. To the economically poor, the home is where one's duty calls—the poor parents, the not-well-to-do relatives. The overtures of this deep concern may be traced in the sacrificial living of the working boys in the big cities, where, though away from home, their thoughts still gravitate towards their families. They never consider it a sacrifice on their part to forego, not only luxuries but often even necessities, for the sake of those whom they have left behind. It may appear to the prudent as the economically weak seeking strength in union.

Marriage is an institution which maintains the indispensable tradition of family life. Unlike the West, in India, it is never one individual marrying another that takes place: you marry *into a family* or marry *from a family*. This means that the first brunette that a boy meets with may not be immediately led to the Registrar's office. The brunette and the boy are those who are going to live together, true, but they would not think of doing it merely according to their own wish. Rather they would defer a great deal to the desires and suggestions of their families. The parents or elders will carefully inquire into not only the present but also the past, tracing history through generations to decide upon the suitability of the bride and the groom. According to the Hindu rites, the astrological forecasts of the parties to a marriage have to be compared and be found *astrologically* agreeable before the marriage can be settled. This practice, strange as it may sound to the Western ear, has this in its favor: that the conditioning influence of the upbringing of the child is taken into account. Nobody can claim to be uninfluenced by his family of origin, and it is pretty fairly certain that the formative influences on an individual have to be clearly reckoned with if a sensible family relationship with him or her is to be anything but a hazardous venture.

The almost complete absence of any kind of dating system, again places on home the function of providing intelligent information about the partner-to-be. As long as young men and women are obliged to live in the absence of interpersonal relationships, even at the university levels, and marriage continues to be a gamble on life and happiness, the only accepted agency that can give authoritative information and analysis is the home.

While by and large the boy or the girl has an increasing say in the matter of his or her marriage, it is still largely one of those decisions where the main actors concede to the weight of supposedly "advisory" opinions which actually have come to be imperative by custom. This is in line with a way of life in general where deference to the elders is heavily institutionalized.

Distinction must, however, be made here between aspects of past-orientation which pertain to the traditional Chinese family life and the Indian life.

In China, the ancients and their worship are such a strong tradition, that the present life is considered a kind of obligation to the past—to please the spirits of the departed. Implicit obedience is imperative when the will of the spirits is invoked. As a consequence, life becomes inflexibly rigid, allowing little possibility of change, since any changes must be sanctioned by those who are departed. It is therefore, a natural sequel to show the utmost deference to the elders, the elders of today being the spirits of tomorrow.

In India, the process is somewhat reversed. Homage to the departed is more a by-product of obedience to the living elders than vice versa. Mother and father are "Visible Gods." Pleasing them becomes, therefore, the duty of the children.

They are taught to worshipfully remember their parents on all important occasions: homage being proper while appearing at an examination, etc. The Hindu Scriptures abound in eulogies of those who have put loyalty to parents above everything else —of how they triumphed over difficulties because they were devoted. It is interesting to observe that the word used to denote loyalty is the same, be it to God, King, Mother or Father —*Bhakti*. The departed are accorded respect as a sequel to the respect given them while alive, the present loyalty leading to that in the future rather than the other way around.

This fundamental difference in character of the two codes of conduct reveals a striking need for divergent approaches to the reorganizing of life in China and India. It is reported that the Red Government has sought to alter many an institution in the present; and it has not left the past untouched either. The huge mounds raised in memory of the ancients have been leveled in order to raise crops. It is not certain what the effect of such demolition will be. Obviously it is not merely a few mounds of earth which are involved in the process; it touches the vital cords of the Chinese life, its very sustenance and protective guide. Known for long-suffering, the Chinese may put up with this moral outrage. But as happens in the awakening of a giant, once disturbed out of its slumber, it may stretch with such might that super-human strength cannot control it. In this context, the terrible discontent, implanted in Chinese minds by the destruction of their revered symbols may culminate in a volcanic eruption of social upheaval.

Mention may be made in this context of how the de-deification of the Japanese Emperor was carried out. Hirohito was not an ordinary man whom the superstition of an Eastern people lifted high above the ordinary realms of conduct and thought. He was more than a symbol. His eminence was not personal. In radically tampering with his personage, it is almost certain that more than the immediate objective of dethroning an empty symbol was achieved. People are persistent in their prejudices, adamant in their refusal to be separated from them.

Take for instance, the value attached to gold as a storage of value even in the mid-twentieth century, where monetary superiority is hardly reckoned in weights of gold, and when the Gold Standard is a game long given up as impractical. Psychologists claim the yellow color to be the reason for gold's significance as a symbol; but why yellow and no other color? Yet, it is still unfashionable to discuss "going off gold:" it is considered somewhat tantamount to going off one's rocker. The world still sticks to gold. If hard-headed monetary authorities can bet their all on a piece of metal of no particular merit in its own right, except those attributed by some kind of prejudice, why should a more ostensibly valid prejudice, and a far more significantly vital one, be denied to a whole people?

It is imperative that advantage must be taken of the lessons of history in regard to the haste of the experiments to refashion the whole thinking of a nation overnight. If the youth in India were to be encouraged to assert their independence and launch out of their traditional moorings of deference to and respect for the older generations, it is almost certain to end up in an abominable situation. If, for instance, the young men were encouraged to go against conservatism at home, and consolidate their inherited holdings or even introduce new machinery, it would mean an eternal conflict in the minds of these young men; because, with all their seeming independence, they never consider themselves as separate from their home of origin, which, despite all its shortcomings, is the custodian of all the traditional values. The fact that they went against the warnings of their parents would continually gnaw the minds of the young men; and no student of sociology needs be told the effect of isolated violations of institutionalized taboos.

In this context of almost involuntary response to someone's else initiative, a vigorous sense of personal responsibility and initiative cannot be built in a day by striking at the root of this responsiveness. No method can ever hope to succeed which starts or attempts mere modification of the responsiveness part of the job. Responsiveness, like the cement at the base of teeth, is a necessary element of cohesion. If it also affords a convenient location for dirt and bacteria, the best cure obviously would not be to remove all the cement: the teeth would fall away. Two important factors that enter into consideration here are: one, that the responsiveness to the older generation has been so thoroughly institutionalized that it is best left alone; and two, it may be a very long time indeed before the youth might be assertive enough to be intellectually independent of the wisdom of their elders.

In other words, to suggest that since the old are too old to be changed from their ways, concentration on the young would deliver the goods, is at best a short-sighted statement. Reference may be made here, to the discussion in Chapter Five of the synthetic nature of the Indian mind. The synthetic nature puts a premium on over-all judgments; and in India, over-all judgments are an everyday necessity. Be it in the matter of marriage, or in the timing of sowing or harvesting, the judgment has to be comprehensive, life itself being a continuing complex of all-embracing situations and not merely isolated instances of individual decisions which could be taken and pursued in separate air-tight compartments. And such judgments being the order of the day, the daily bread of the people's way of living, wisdom has priority over intellect. The ball rolls back to the old men and the older generation. Their pronouncements are the directives for the activity of youth. The older generation makes decisions like the veteran Field-Marshalls, and onward goes the youth like fiery generals.

It is in modifying the decisions of the "Field Marshalls" that adult education becomes relevant. However, it must be pointed out here that a system of education which has as its aim imparting only a knowledge of the alphabet is next to useless. It will only repeat the horrible mistake of the English system of education which was thrust upon the country as a by-product of the need to recruit a clerical staff. *The adults are not to be re-educated.* If poise in the judgment of contemporary issues is one of the objects of a wholesome education, the adults are already highly educated: for instance, reference may be made to the discussion above, of how they handled their votes in the first election. The objective of adult education should be to provide an *extension* service for their already acute judgments which would take care of the new facets of human activity, be they political, economic or technological, that take place day by day, hour by hour. It is only such an ability as this which will correct the isolationist, closed nature of the present decisions of the older generation arising mostly out of an absence of encounters with, or inadequate encounters with, the rapidly increasing complicated circumstances of life in contemporary times.

This introductory material on the units of power and organization in Indian life, it is hoped, will enable those interested to see that there is a definite and intangible force which holds the old and the young generations together in the changes and chances of this fleeting world. Any untimely upsetting of this relationship, arising out of even the highest objectives, is bound to completely frustrate attempts at social reconstruction. It has got to begin on human levels; and human levels mean the units of power and organization operative in the life of the society. The mistake had been committed, time and time again, of overlooking this inalienable bond between the old and the new with the according drastic results. Proselytizing on an individual level just does not take root in a soil where life is always familial. The results of stray individual acceptances of Jesus Christ as Saviour and Lord have been doomed to die in the wilderness of ostracization, both by the immediate family and the society. Even as salvation is a personal matter, so are agricultural reform or farming practices. The individual has to be reached: he has to make the personal decision; but for that decision to hold, the smallest unit, the family, must also participate fully.

CHAPTER EIGHT

ARE FACTS SYMBOLS, OR
SYMBOLS FACTS?

The mixed marriage of Indian instincts and British manners—unresolved conflicts of imposed cultural change—the plethora of symbols in Indian life—the philosophical disposition challenged by literalisms: (1) nationalism (2) communism (3) Americanism—should the evils of industrial revolution be repeated in India?—creative philosophy and philosophic creativity.

A PHILOSOPHY OF ACTION for India today should address itself to the baffling choice with which the Indian family is confronted. Hinduism teaches them to treat facts as symbols: communism teaches that symbols are facts. No sooner is the entire family persuaded to think in terms of a new way of living than this baffling choice arises.

The peasant and his family had for ages seen facts as symbols. The ever-rotating wheel of life and death stood as an eternal symbol of the continuity of life and time in self-perpetuation. Its meaning, was not for them to question. They knew only that in and through their lives, through the many privations and few joys, was symbolized the great Truth of existence. They were content to leave it as a mystery fit to be pondered upon by the holy men. From time to time they were assured that their miseries were an illusion (*Maya*), and that

the goal of their lives was in the losing of their souls in the
Ultimate (*Nirvana*). They could afford the sublime unconcern
that they had for all material things in the world, because their
chief end was to achieve consummation in the ultimate. If they
were hungry, why, it was the result of their past *Karma*, their
past deeds and misdeeds. It was part of the divine dispensation,
unalterable in its execution, unquestionable as to its wisdom.

And now they are told that there are different ways of
ordering their lives.

This is not the first time that they have encountered an altogether different manner of living: in the 1600's, the British
came. They had had predecessors, but they had not remained
long enough to make a people so used to long periods of history sit up and take notice. But not so the British. They brought
about changes in dress, manners and communication: changes
so radical and all-permeating that the noted historian Arnold
Toynbee writes about the conflict in the Hindu soul:

> India is a whole world in herself; she is a society of the same
> magnitude as our Western society; and she is one of the great
> non-Western societies that has been, not merely attacked and
> hit, but over-run and conquered outright by Western arms,
> but ruled after that, by Western administrators . . . Whatever
> may be the relief that Hindu souls are going to find for them-
> selves eventually, it seems clear that, for them, there can be
> no relief from the impact of our Western civilization by
> opening themselves to the influence of Communism; for Com-
> munism—a Western heresy adopted by an ex-Orthodox
> Christian Russia—is just as much part and parcel of the
> Graceo—Judaic heritage as the Western way of life is, and the
> whole of this cultural tradition is alien to the Hindu spirit. [1]

This conflict in which the noted historian sees the portents
of a blow-up has been the direct result of a half-marriage
between two distinctly different cultures without adequate
regard for the problems of adaptation involved. The torment

that Toynbee refers to in the Hindu soul came from quite an odd kind and number of sweeping changes. It included in its broad span, the abhorrence on the part of the Brahmin for the intrusion of a white rectangular piece of material which dissolves in water and produces a foam which is used to mar the celestial purity of his holy clothes.

Pet theories and medicines rooted in ignorant superstition were exploded. Education was thrown open to one and all, the Brahmin no longer holding the sole key to knowledge.

Nor were the changes confined to the Brahmins. The farmer father who for so long had remained unquestionable overlord of all that he surveyed, master of his servants, found that his beck and call no longer brought forth the same set of willing hands whose pleasure it had been to do and die and never to question. The organic bond of master-servant (virtually, master-slave) relationship no longer remained the same even as the methods of manuring did not. Strict vegetarians, whose herbivorous nature had scriptural sanction, found themselves handling animal matter on the land to make it more productive, and if there were lapses to meat-tasting, why, that was one of the evil results of an alien culture.

In short, the little amenities of life that the West brought with it, from washing soap to steam engines, were shaking the entire social structure to its very substratum, rudely uprooting the system of symbols which that pattern signified. It was far more than a few metal images that were involved as in most instances of Moghul invasion: it was the proud announcement of one invader, "I do not want to be remembered as the Mohammed of Ghazny who *sold* idols but who *broke* them." The British were not merely selling or breaking a few idols: they were consummating a destruction of the widest sweep, which was ruthlessly breaking images more precious than idols of gold—images constituted of values, manners and customs held inviolable and sacred across the ages. After putting down these mighty institutions from their throne, the West exalted alien institutions.

A desolation so intimate as this, which desecrated the entire range of fond prejudices that a whole people had cherished, preserved and passed on for successive generations, will admittedly be of more than skin-deep consequence. Two hundred years are by no means adequate time in which the consequences could be tested, proved or accepted. And the musing discontent, fuming and vigorously alive, even as a volcano, is a very common feature of cultures when their future is violently threatened. It might be interesting to recall how that eminent authoress depicts the undying spirit of the "Old Guard" in her immortal story which describes how an entire civilization had "Gone With the Wind."

> Starving is good enough for us. It ought to be good enough for you" was the way the Old Guard felt. Many ex-Confederate soldiers, knowing the frantic fear of men who saw their families in want, were more tolerant of former comrades who had changed political colors in order that their families might eat. But not the women of the Old Guard, and the women were the implacable and inflexible power behind the social throne. The Lost Cause was stronger, dearer now in their hearts than it had ever been at the heights of its glory. It was a fetish now. Everything about it was sacred, the graves of the men who had died for it, the battle fields, the torn flags, the crossed sabres in their halls, the fading letters from the front, the veterans. These women gave no aid, comfort or quarter to the late enemy . . .
>
> My dear Miss Melly, it is always a privilege and a pleasure to be in your home, for you—and ladies like you—are the hearts of all of us, all that we have left. They have taken the flower of our manhood, and the laughter of our young women. They have broken our health, uprooted our lives and unsettled our habits. They have ruined our prosperity, set us back fifty years, and placed too heavy a burden on the shoulders of our boys who should be in school and our old men who should be sleeping in the sun. But we will build

back, because we have hearts like yours to build upon. And
as long as we have them, the Yankees can have the rest! [2]

It is these undying embers which the zealous reformer over-
looks on a hasty glance at superficialities. Who knows that the
horrible agonies of the ancient spirit of China would not come
alive into active assertion of its own on a most unexpected day,
throwing out entirely the enveloping regime which so blatantly
disregarded almost every institution that the Chinese people
had learned to love and rever, nay to worship?

In the millions of years that have gone by there have been
woven into the pattern of life innumerable symbols which persist long after, and live far beyond, what the actual facts themselves can signify. In many a farm family, even today, the
plough, used from time immemorial, must be kept in the same
old corner where it had been kept by the great-grandfather.
The same number of men and women must work in the fields.
The traditional ceremonial occasions when the servants (in
Travancore, family servants refer to themselves while address-
ing the family masters as *"Adiyan"*—a term signifying bond
slavehood rather than mere servantship) bring *Karzscha* (homage, offering) and the masters acknowledge them with returns
in kind, have all to be preserved in the same form as they
were, with all the regalia. Entirely disproportionate to the
magnitudes involved, the implements, ceremonies and number
of laborers stand for the presetige of the family, and for all
that it stood for in the years that went by. A *Karzscha* is not
looked upon as an exchange of goods of equivalent value, but
rather, as a symbol of the inflexible caste system, ordained and
sustained by inscrutable laws. It is the institution that survives
generations: men may come and men may go, but the symbols
go on for ever.

The worship of the earth as the source of blessing is not a
mere hangover of the ancient days of animistic religion. In
fact, any learned Hindu will tell you that he is not worship-

ing the idol that is before him—be it the personification of the goddess of earth, or the sun god or the goddess of wrath or of learning. Once when a prime minister of a small state asked a sage why he worshipped idols, he pointed to a picture of the king hanging on the wall. "Put it down," he said. Reluctantly, the Prime Minister removed the picture from the wall in the presence of the king. "Stamp on it," was the next order from the sage. The Prime Minister would not. "Why," said the sage, "it is only a picture. It is not your king. Then why do you hesitate? We worship not the image that you see before your eyes but what it symbolizes."

It is these undying symbols peeping out of every crack and crevice of the social structure that have been mercilessly attacked by technology and technological devices. This dire disregard of the traditional manner of living has touched off a volcano of social upheaval whose simmering fire has burned and broiled within for a long, long time.

In Indian life, there is a plethora of symbols. A large number of codes of conduct are built around the symbols. For instance, you never step into a house with your left foot; you never hand over anything to anybody but with your right hand; you never go on a journey on certain days; and then again, when you start your journey, you should look for the signs; if you happen to sight the back of a cow as the first thing on your journey, your journey is auspicious; on august occasions, the number and tone of the noise produced by the lizard as well as the direction from which the noise originated, have the most amazing determinative effect on the course and conduct of affairs; certain kinds of serpents are not venomous, but they indicate significant directives for human life; if a serpent is seen in a particular spot; if it came out of a particular hole at a particular time, halfway between dark and dawn, at midday or dusk it is meaningful—every one of these details connotes distinct messages for the people; maybe they have not paid their vows; maybe they have transgressed some code of behavior. The serpents which transmit these mysterious messages are said to be harmless. For instance, even if a child happens to stamp on one, it is said that the serpent would not bite. As soon as the people express some kind of response, for instance when somebody says that he will pay off the vows at such and such a time, the serpent goes away. Just as mysteriously as it made its appearance, it is gone.

A surprising degree of kindness to animals is one of the results of this bundle of superstitions. This again, comes directly from the religious belief of the Hindu in reincarnation. In a context of reward and punishment, the individual assumes a new kind of life in the next incarnation. Wicked living will be rewarded by being condemned to be born as a lower animal. Who knows—the cow that you respect may be your own form in your next life, or, it might be some ancestor of yours still doing penance for past misdeeds. In the busy streets of Calcutta, which was the second largest city in the old British Empire, and which has a present population close to half that of New York, the world's largest city, if there is one animal that can walk in the streets with impunity and safety, it is the cow. You hear of men being run over, children being knocked down, women being involved in traffic accidents; but never the cow. Yet the most flagrant violations of traffic rules are made by these mute animals, whose muteness is their very safeguard. Its frail frame, by itself, would never have done the trick; it is the eternal symbolism that it connotes in its body that commands the worshipful respect which is continuously offered.

The cow is the symbol of productivity; and so is the woman. When a cow is entrusted to someone to be fed and taken care of—as is done in middle class families—it must be the woman in the family who hands it over. It is more often the woman of the house who milks the cow. This is not merely an aspect of the division of labor, but rather the direct or indirect result of the symbolic nature of productivity of womanhood. Again when the harvest is brought home, it is the woman's role o honor to direct the storage in the respective granaries; it is she, who is the representative of the goddess of good fortune, who should handle the symbol of fruition—the ripe rice from the fields. Successful housewives are referred to as *Lakshmi*, the goddess of wealth. In the Hindu family, the woman occupies a unique position as the director of religious ceremonies. And, as was mentioned earlier, the mother and father are "Visible Gods."

But women occupy a subordinate position in the home as well as social circles. With all the above worshipfulness associated with them, they are to fulfill their glorious role in and to the extent of their almost servile obedience to their husbands. To the wife, the husband is the Visible God, devotion to whom is absolute and inexorable. And she, the symbol of prosperity, looks to him for fulfillment. Man is still the master in the family.

Introduction of machinery means a complete upsetting of facts which would immediately challenge effectively every one of these symbols.

Bulldozers would mean that the good old bullocks which the father had grown up with since childhood would no longer be the means of tilling. Pasturization would mean that the cow which supplies the milk is no longer the same baby calf which was the son's pet and the daughter's delight, but some member of an unidentifiable mass. If the cow becomes a mass productive agency, it stands to lose the individuality which had made it an object of worship throughout the ages. The mechanical storage of grain would dispense with the luck, or lack of luck, of the housewife in providing food; it would then depend on the capacity of storage facilities and the amount of grain in the field. No longer those long hours which the farmer would spend in his own small plot of land of hallowed memory, watching the growth of every little blade even as a mother watches the teeth of her baby; the machine takes care of the timing of planting, of growing and of harvesting.

Along with the complete loss of the individual touch comes the impersonality of the application of power. Turning on a switch is not an operation suitable for the man of the family who was the symbol of fulfillment to his dependents. He might be handy in repairs; but for the operation of the machinery, there will be the instruction booklet. All the majesty of traditional land endeavor suddenly becomes totally irrelevant. Imagine the impudence of the small bit of steel that has undermined the wisdom of the ages!

Again, the great genie of technical equipment would mean that there is no more room for resignation or irresponsibility. If the harvest is poor, if the waters are insufficient, it is no longer because of insufficient propitiation to the weather gods, but because the men did not build up adequate supplies. To a people who have been used to a glorious resignation to the immutable wisdom of an inscrutable destiny, there is the sudden news that they are the architects of their own fortune. It is no longer what has been willed for them that matters, but what they have been prepared to work for.

This could easily smack both of sacrilege and subversion —sacrilege in religious sanction and subversion in social life. For, there is the deposing of gods, gods who reigned supreme over rain, shine and life, and there is the deification of man and material instead. There is subversion in social life because it is no longer plausible to continue the mute reign of hierarchic overlordship that has been the rule of ages.

It is little wonder that the workers of the Industrial Revolution Era fought so frantically against the evil demon of machinery. In their case, it was a matter of their bread being taken away. In the present instance, bread itself would not be so prominent as the sacrilege involved and the subversive potential of the move in regard to the pattern of social living.

The radical change involved in the process is from the philosophical disposition to see facts as mere symbols to a literalism which sees symbols as facts.

Bernard Shaw, in his *Man and Superman*, mentions two kinds of games that are played: one, the game we play; and two, the game that is played on us. To the Indian peasant, because of his philosophic disposition, life is entirely a game that is played on him—be it his own past deeds and misdeeds, the virtue or otherwise of his ancestors, or the fury or mercy of the gods which has motivated the moves of the game. The moment he is offered the mastery over technical devices, he is imbued with a knowledge which, in its imperfect novelty, deludes him into believing that his entire life is a game that he alone plays.

It is interesting to note that Karl Marx found it fit to use a neo-Renaissance concept of the mechanism of history. Renaissance seated man in the seventh heaven of glory. Crowned in glory, man would dare to command the waves until he would learn, like good old King Canute's courtiers, that there were limits in and to his universe. But the burning of man's fingers by the fire of power, mechanical, technical or political, is an essential prerequisite in a world where he is created free. But he assumes the sovereign role of the drama, forgetting that his royal plumage is not of his own creation, but is rather, like his freedom, a gift along with his life. And there are innumerable tales of celebrities, who like King Nebuchadnezzar, have had to eat grass like oxen and be wetted by the dew of heaven for seven years before realizing that great Babylon was not entirely their own creation.[3]

Not long after the Renaissance, which sang of the glory of man, came the unpleasant realization of Rousseau, that, "Man is born free, but he is everywhere in chains!" Hobbes found the life of man in the state of nature to be "short, nasty, brutish." Why did this desperation follow so fast on the heels of the acclamation of man's crowning glory?

George Orwell, in his beautiful story, *Animal Farm*, depicts what happens to the animals of a farm when they succeeded in overthrowing their master. In their new power, they ordered their lives according to Ten Commandments of their own, beginning with "All two-footers are evil." The victorious revolution soon produced its own leadership—pigs. The company of pigs acted as the brain of the community. The animals built much technical equipment of their own, including a huge windmill. Throughout the days of continuous struggle, sacrifice and hard work, the constant consolation to the animals' aching backs and starving stomachs was the promise of future days of luxury. These days never came.

The story goes on to describe the changes that came over the Ten Commandments which were a direct outcome of the compromise with their enemy, humans, that the pig leaders were continuously making. At last, the animals got restive with what was happening to their hard-won freedom. They heard an uproar coming from the quarters of the pigs. Peeping through the windows, they found that a big banquet was in progress with men and pigs seated on either side of the table. There were speeches and breaking of glasses, drinking and merry-making. Then suddenly the watchers noticed the change: the pigs were on two legs and the men on four—*it was no longer possible to tell the one from the other.*

One of the morals that could be drawn from this satire is that of what happens when power is not accompanied with commensurate wisdom. Bacon was only too accurate when he said that great empires and small minds go ill together. With all their vast wealth, the inanimate empire has to be steered properly by great men: men who are greater than the powers they wield themselves. In the case of the animal farm, the pigs had the technical know-how and organizing ability, discipline and public order, but they never knew what they could do with power. And power will drive you if you do not drive it. The pigs could not drive power; so power drove them back into a worse state than that which they experienced under human bondage: a state where even their previous guides, humans, lost their moorings also.

Man, rising in his glory in the Renaissance period, found himself in possession of a force far greater than his own regulatory powers. When Rousseau said that, born free, man was everywhere in chains, he did not realize that man was not *born* but *created* free. Vaulting back from the individualism of Hobbes, Locke and Rousseau, political philosophy made the offering of individual freedom at the altar first of the nation, and then of the masses in general. Hegel probably never thought of the twist that would be given to his dialectic to form the excellent framework of the materialistic interpretation of class wars. Naturally enough, wars can not be fought single-handed; they are manned by classes. In a war, discipline cannot be enforced unless obedience is unquestioned. Herein is the logical outgrowth of the political philosophy of the interlude of Nebuchadnezzar's grass-eating: man had put himself on a pinnacle, and before he could realize what had happened, was in the dust, eating his own pride under the iron hands of masters to whom he had relegated his destiny.

In this context of immense power and noncommensurate wisdom which is a recurrent situation in history, the Indian peasant faces various proffered alternatives to his own philosophical disposition.

During the fight for independence, the glorious past of the country was understandably a source of inspiration to the Indians. But if the same theme is to be reiterated twelve years after the achievement of political emancipation, it does not do too much credit to the wide perspective that ought to have relegated the narrative of ancient glory to its proper dimension. An almost vehement recitation of past achievements would suggest the absence of any achievements at the present. The reference to the past during discussion of the present may suggest an ill-concealed attempt at compensating for some inferiority complex.

If inferiority is the motivation for persistently living in the past, its harmful influence in national life is with reference to its substituting a short-term view of the historical process for a truly long-term one.

To suggest that national prestige in the present is the most immediate issue of contemporary history, is to challenge the philosophical disposition which reckons facts of history as symbols of life itself, and to exalt current events to the status of ultimate happenings—or, to consider symbols as facts.

This short-sighted consideration of historical events, which are essentially symbolic of life as the ultimate facts in themselves has ample precedence in history—from the Greeks who decided to go into all the inhabited earth (*oekomene*) to spread their civilization among barbarians, to the Super Race of Adolf Hitler.

Indian nationalism, even if it does stand in need of a tendency to assume finality of its interpretation and role in history, is thus not unique. However, sinning in good company does not condone sin. Rigorous reappraisal of the philosophy of Indian nationalism is called for: an appraisal which will serve to throw into sharp relief whatever tendencies there may be swerving the philosophic disposition of the people toward a literalistic view of history. Such an appraisal would also serve to clarify the essentials of a philosophic disposition. Only when the people know clearly what their own heritage is, will they be able to weigh the relevance of the alternate approaches to a view of life.

This clarity of concept is called for even more urgently in understanding the nature of the communist alternative.

To the Hindu, his existence is symbolic of the ever-rotating wheel of life. The vicissitudes of his existence are passing trifles in view of the consummation his life is destined to achieve in successive reincarnations, and in the ultimate losing of its identity in the Infinite.

This other-worldly view of the Hindu is completely reversed in the materialistic interpretation of history. According to this plank of communist (more correctly, Marxian) analysis, there is no reincarnation, no life after death. The duty of the hour, the work of winning the revolution, is paramount. Any means is welcome: all is fair in revolution.

Obviously, the Hindu finds the alternative unsatisfactory from the point of view of his philosophic disposition. The jump from other-worldly orientation to this-worldly orientation, from future-orientation to present-orientation, from infinity-orientation to immediate-orientation poses an unceremonious *volte face*.

On the philosophical plane, these gymnastics remain repulsive. But man lives not only by philosophy, but also by bread. And bread is promised by the communist alternative.

How long the challenge of the communist alternative will remain a menace is dependent on how quickly the imperative social revolution will take place through evolutionary processes. There is definitely a headstart provided by the fact that the views on life presented by the alternative are radically opposed to those of the people's deep-rooted beliefs. This headstart must be expanded by engineering community activities *simultaneously* on physical and intellectual planes.

American technical aid to India is administered through people who have a national background of their own. The American background is definitely not the most passive element that enters into the administration of technical assistance. As Nehru pointed out in his address to the German Foreign Policy Association, there is a discernible missionary attitude to spread the American Way of Life. Since this endeavor also bids for the acceptance of the Indian, it is relevant to consider it from the point of view of the Indian's philosophic disposition.

What is Americanism, or the American Way of Life?

The American Way of Life is, at bottom, a spiritual structure, a structure of ideas and ideals, of aspirations and values, of beliefs and standards; it synthesizes all that commends itself to the American as the right, the good, and the true in actual life. It embraces such seemingly incongruous elements as sanitary plumbing and freedom of opportunity, Coca-Cola and an intense faith in education—*all felt as moral questions* relating to the proper way of life . . .

The American Way of Life is individualistic, dynamic, pragmatic. It affirms the supreme value and dignity of the individual; it stresses incessant activity on his part, for he is never to rest but is always to be striving to "get ahead"; it defines an ethic of self-reliance, merit and character, and *judges by achievement*: *"deeds, not creeds" are what count.* [4] (italics supplied)

The feeling that sanitary plumbing, Coca-Cola and an intense faith in education are all moral questions indicates the ardor of the religion: when the masses in India are seen to live in unhygienic circumstances, it is not counted as a shortcoming in modern living conveniences, but as a *"moral defect,"* on a par with irreligion, caste rigidity, and the absence of American representative democracy."

The peasant in India is used to making moral issues out of many events and relationships in daily, personal life. But matters of food and drink have a long way to go before becoming burning issues to him. The ethos of his life has little respect for "mundane" matters such as food and drink; maybe he has been obliged to be stoic in this respect owing to the poverty of the country.

Whatever be the reasons, moral issues made out of the food-and-drink platform are not likely to succeed in inducing the people of India to incorporate Americanism in their lives. The communists have a different platform, also emphasizing food-and-drink. Theirs, however, does not concern "moral" questions, but rather matters of subsistence. The philosophic peasant can also be hungry: and food will interest him. But good food, as a moral issue, is a novelty which is not likely to impress him.

Judgment by achievement, i.e., "deeds, not creeds," is likely to grate severely with the Indian temperament. He will respect achievement, but creeds are very important to him. His very life is so intricately interwoven with creeds that he would rather err on the side of creeds rather than deeds.

Material prosperity, in the mind of the Indian, is linked inversely with true religion. He is prone to think that it is as near to impossible for a rich man to be religious as for a camel to pass through a needle's eye. The burden of proof is on the American exponent of his religious convictions; his material advancement charges him in the eyes of the Indian as one who has a business-like interest in the Chairman of the Board of Trustees of Universe Incorporated.

The American Way of Life as an alternative proffered in an effort to supplant the bid of communism in deflecting the Indian from his philosophic disposition is thus questioned by the Indian. His questioning is reflected in the acceptance speech of the Democratic Party's nominee to the Presidency of the United States, Adlai E. Stevenson, when he said:

> There is a spiritual hunger in the world today and it cannot be satisfied by material things alone. Our forebears came here to worship God. We must not let our aspirations so diminish that *our worship becomes rather of bigness—bigness of material achievement.* [5] (italics supplied)

The italics indicate the nature of the Indian's questioning of the American Way of Life which he is told is the sure foundation for successful living.

The wistful Indian again takes a look at the American Way of Life that has already been revealed to have entirely different ideas about what is moral and what is not from his own views, an entirely different approach to the meaning of achievement, and a halo of material bigness around even his religious worship. What is the nature of the American's religion?

Americans fill the houses of worship, but their conceptions, standards, and values, their institutions and loyalties, bear a strangely ambiguous relation to the teachings that the churches presumably stand for . . . Of the very same Americans who so overwhelmingly affirm their belief in God and their membership in the historic churches, a majority also affirm, without any sense of incongruousness, that their religion has little to do with their politics, or business affairs, except to provide an additional sanction and drive. Most of the other activities of life—education, science, entertainment— could be added to the list; they too apparently operate under their own rules, with religion invoked as a "spiritual" embelishment and a useful sustaining force. *This is not felt as in any case a disparagement of religion;* it is merely America's way of defining for itself the place of religion and the church in the total scheme of things. But this way of looking at things is precisely the way of secularism, for what is secularism but the practice of the absence of God in the affairs of life? [6] (italics supplied)

One of the big differences between the Indian and the American attitude toward religion is that if the former does these things, he is likely to feel that his doings are a disparagement of religion. This feeling would arise out of his concept of secularism, which is always dignity-wise, lower than nonsecularism. Secularism may be defined as a conditioning context of human activity, limiting itself to finite dimensions. Nonsecularism would be characterized by its quality of constantly evaluating itself in the context of eternal contemporaneousness.

Thus, the Indian's religion is not what it should be; but he is at least conscious of it, and does make pronouncements on the necessity for self-evaluation in the context of the eternal contemporaneousness of the inexorable laws of life. He is confronted with two great contenders for his soul—communism and Americanism. Neither of them seem able to cope with his thirst for a philosophy of action. Even if he were to accept parts of either, or both, which is very likely, deep problems of the creation of conflicts and their resolution, dating back to the tensions created from the 1600's on, raise pointed questions, the neglect of which can only be at the peril of the sanity of the mind of India.

India is industrializing herself. Americans, British, Germans and Russians are helping in the process of building industries and mechanizing agriculture in India. In addition to the religious values and the philosophical disposition involved in this process, there is also the question of the social aspects of mechanization.

In the Indian context, the problem would be of a similar nature to that currently being faced by the industrially advanced nations. "Ministers in Industry," which was started as a small movement in France by a handful of Catholic priests who found it necessary to obey God by identifying themselves with the workers to whom they were ministering, even participating in their strikes and other mundane details of industrial life, has sent out its ripples to the different parts of the globe. A zealous hunt is being made today. Object: to bring the industrial laborer back to the church, to tell him that he is counted not as a mere cog in a machine but as a son of God. Young ministers go and work with the laborers in summer in the United States, so that they might know more of the situations faced by the laborer in industry. All over, there is a hunt, a divine hunt, for the laborer, the worker in industry.

It might be rather unorthodox to suggest that this frantic hunt on the part of the church today is at least partly the result of overlooking the vital problems of symbolism in the heat of industrialization.

One of the important modifications, it may be recalled, that the Industrial Revolution brought about was the rise of the factory. Leaving their own homes, people had to work under larger roofs, with other men, the only common bond among them being "skilled *hands*." The moment the workers became "hands," they found themselves doomed to the companionship of powerplants and steam engines, which cannot speak, nor be spoken to. But man, as Hazlitt says, "is the only animal that laughs and weeps, for he is the only animal that is struck by the difference between what things are and what they ought to be." This means that he has a sense of what ought to be. Those industrial workers of the Industrial Revolution Era had an idea of what ought to be. Their own immediate past told them of their own homes in which they worked, in which they were fathers, brothers and sons, and not hands. When the continuity of the emotional security at home was broken, still men had the faculty of weeping and laughing. The machines were inanimate; and for centuries to come, until the time of Robert Owen and of Factory Acts, the worker, who was thrown out of his moorings and enslaved by a force which endowed him with a new kind of power, could not speak about his own hopes and fears, either to the inanimate machinery or to the impersonal system.

When crying was wasted in the wilderness, it took a bitter turn. Piteous groanings turned in upon the groaner: they were not going to put up with it. Hideous laughter took its place; a laughter which scotched any suggestions of love by its sheer sarcasm of mute contemptuousness. The industrial worker found that he was not wanted except as a by-product of impersonal machinery in a system which continuously battled with itself in its own covetousness and greed. Life was pointless, an endless succession of sirens, wheel-turning and tool-making, a mad fury signifying nothing.

During those days, when the worker could never unburden his grief over the broken symbolisms in his own life, there were men who tried to figure out a way for the airing and redressing of these evils. Karl Marx was one of these men who were moved by the relentless rigidity that dehumanized the individual. He had an idea: "Working men of the world, unite. You have nothing but your chains to lose!"

Working men all over the world heard the cry; it has been echoing and re-echoing ever since.

In the mid-twentieth century, the church comes forward to proclaim the Love which saw the worker as a son of God.

The worker is weary; he no longer cries: his distrust in man and God is now more hideous laughter than piteous moaning. He has other systems to care for him.

History can repeat itself; what happened in England can happen in India. But must it be the hard way? Should the Indian peasant undergo the frustrating uprooting from the symbolism of his life, which saw facts as symbols, to the Communistic literalism of symbols as facts, before he recognizes that he is *created free* for *freedom in love?*

CHAPTER NINE

FAITH PLANK OF A PHILOSOPHY
OF ACTION

*Possible outcome of a new orientation—love that makes life
a worship—a dynamic faith: "If I slip Thou dost not fall"—a
new view of history—creative participation.*

IF INDIA IS TO BE SPARED the avoidable, ugly pains of the Industrial Revolution of the eighteenth century, she needs to find
and formulate a dynamic faith. This faith should satisfy her
philosophic disposition; it should also encourage realism in
regard to the oncoming mechanization of her life. Once India
has a faith which meets the demands of her complicated life,
certain consequences would follow:

First, on the individual level, there can no longer be the
sublime unconcern for the fruits of one's labor, the responsibility for which has so long been willingly shouldered by Fate
or the disposition of the gods.

Second, on the social level, the individual is bound to be
emancipated from subjection to the family. Even as its
economic counterpart, the Matriarchal System, which pooled
the resources of all the constituent units and divided them
among the members, could not hold out under the stress of
increasing numbers as well as resurgent leadership from the
bottom, the predominantly familial concept of fame and for-

tune will also be substantially modified by an increasingly distinctive individual accent.

Third, the emanicipation of the individual would mean greater freedom in marriage. The bride will not be just married into or out of a *family*, but be married by and to an *individual*. It may still be a long way from the bride marrying her husband: the groom will continue to be the active partner in the courtship.

Fourth, this change in the pattern of living and marriage necessarily calls for providing particular attention to the old; under the existing practices, the parents live with the children one by one, in turn, or at will. It is a prerogative and a most sacred duty, willingly attended to. Every wish of the old folks, even when they are adamantly obstinate, is either fulfilled or at least deferred to. When marriage and new families take their distinctive, necessarily individualistic turn, the organic nature of the family concept would stand to change. In the place of new additions to the old tree, it becomes a new tree altogether; and it then is quite optional whether or not they graft the old folks at home to it.

Fifth, the emancipation of the individual is bound to improve the status of the younger generation. Specifically, this would mean increased freedom in school and college life in the sphere of boy-girl relationships.

Think of the immense sources of power and creativity that will be released by this process of individual emancipation! Men and women exploring new avenues of achievement, no longer bound and restrained by fatalistic resignation; boys and girls mingling freely as is natural for them to do, not having to be ashamed of their natural appetites; older men and women losing their edge of arrogance because they live under a new kind of human relationship—not one where arrogance is king, but where sweetness is what becomes their venerable heads most: it will be the beautiful picture of the awakening of a nation from its slumber under benumbing influences!

Immediately there arises the question of handling this re-surgent power in the body of the nation. The emotional adoles-cence of a nation, arising out of a liberation from repressions of all kinds, is not entirely dissimilar from the problems of puberty in the life of an individual. In both the cases, freedom is the keyword. If repressed, it could, in the case of the indi-vidual, raise problems of inhibition; if licensed, it would ruin the life concerned.

Jung, in his discussion of "The Love Problem of the Stu-dent" makes a beautiful point on the role of love when he says:

> Love is not a cheap matter; let us therefore not cheapen it . . .
> Sexuality released as sexuality is brutish. But as an expression
> of love sexuality is hallowed. Never ask therefore what a man
> does, but how he does it. Does he act from love and in the
> spirit of love, then he serves a god, and whatever he may do;
> it is not our business to judge, for it is ennobled. [1]

Now, what does love mean in this context? One of the important elements that Jung stresses is its self-obligatory nature. The self involved is not subjugated: it is not lost in the union with the other. On the other hand, in losing itself, it finds itself. When Jung speaks of "serving a god," he does not probe further into the indispensable nature of this god. If it is a god with a small letter, certainly this is no unique obli-gation. It could be any one of the infinite number of non-human powers which could be blanketed under the non-human category "god." In fact, according to the use of the term, there is an open possibility of other gods contending for the worship of this devotee and thereby causing trouble. Then it would be a matter to be decided by the strength of the contending gods. It would also largely depend upon the preparedness of the individual concerned for entertaining these rival claims. There is a very real possibility of a conflict between the god of love and of lust. In fact, being very close cousins, it is a hard job to distinguish between love and lust.

This suggestion of close similarity brings us to a recognition the inestimable service done by Freud in fighting the human inhibitions of centuries. His contribution, pertinent to the discussion here, is the affirmation that sex is the basic source of all human activity. This would mean that both lust and love are products of the same primeval force. When once the world outlived the Victorian Era, the natural reaction to an unnatural repression bounced over to the other extreme, verging on licentiousness. Now India is somewhat less inhibited than were the Victorians, but if it is not certain just what society it is choosing for its format, its "god," the change could easily be fraught with the costly consequences of licentiousness in the name of freedom.

If love and lust are so close, and therefore Jung's terminology of a "god" of love is inadequate because it raises the possibility of a simultaneous "god" of lust contending for human devotion, what could be the alternative?

The love that one may serve, and yet be free, should both bring out the best in a person, and should be inexorable in its demands without being covetous of the entire individual. Even a mother's love, while willing to offer its own person for the sake of her child, would find it extremely hard to be displaced in its possessive affection. In the lower rungs of life, these two elements are simultaneously exhibited in the hen fighting for its chicken, the snake hissing against any seemingly potential attackers of its young ones, or in the cow vigorously kicking the air around to keep watch over her new-born calf. It would offer its best for the sake of the child; but it would not part with its child for the most priceless possession in the world.

If even mother's love is not above creeping possessiveness, it loses its claim to be the Love that makes Life a Worship. And the Indian masses, faced with the allurement of material plentitude, and looking back wistfully at the spiritual heritage of the ages, look for some power transcending the troubles of the present and uplifting them not *from* but *in* the vicissitudes of their day, beckoning them to a glorious vision which will make life a worship. This power must surpass the essence of the wisdom of the ages that has sustained their forebearers in the calamities of their day; this power must be able to transform their own lives into something that can rise above the turmoil of the day. If even the love of the mother, who is one of the "Visible Gods," cannot provide this transforming, transcending power, what else conceivably can?

> Love has more than one element in common with religious conviction; it demands an unconditioned attitude and it expects complete surrender. Only that believer who yields himself wholly to his god partakes of the manifestation of divine grace. Similarly, love reveals its highest mysteries and wonder only to him who is capable of unconditioned surrender and loyalty of feeling. Because this is so hard, few indeed of mortal men can boast of achieving it. But just because the most devoted and the truest love is also the most beautiful let no man seek that which could make love easy. He is a sorry knight of his lady who recoils from the difficulty of love. Love is like God: both give themselves only to their bravest knights. [2]

To the highly philosophic Indian, "easy" devotion is never the best means of fulfilling his life. If he were to be told that a few minutes of "positive thinking" would see him through life in all its perils and glory he would cast a painful look at his own past which is so full of formulae recited or applied, and the present in which is offered the challenge of a new formula, Dialectical Materialism, as the talisman for all his problems. No, these alternatives are weighed in the balance and found sadly wanting: they do not deserve the precious human soul of India.

This power must be creative. It must be inexorable in its demands for absolute loyalty. It should create freedom in man.

A freedom that can emancipate the individual, without becoming a pretense for licentiousness, is the only one which would help in the matter. It should spring from that celestial mainspring of Love with a capital L; the Love that seeketh not its own, coveteth not, hoping always for the best; the Love which can say "He must grow, but I must decrease;" the Love in which life and sorrow so uniquely mingle; the Love that wears the most unusual crown of thorns; the Love so amazing, so divine, which does *not* demand my life, my soul or my all, but to which the whole realm of earth, if offered as a present would be so incomparably inconspicuous that I can offer nothing more than myself—and I dare not offer any less.

This freedom tells me that my appetites are nothing of which I need be ashamed; but it also tells me that I violate the rules of the game with my partners the moment I treat them in thought or word or deed as anything other than equal persons—equal in the sight of our Creator who is continuously watching our game, not as a Judge, but as a Friend. His friendship is so transforming that I can ill-afford to preserve my disposition to the rights of myself for myself: yes, even to myself. My time, my talents, my ambitions—every one of them is lifted to a higher plane far beyond the mundane atmosphere of self-will; and when they are dead to me, when I no longer try to put my own label on them, I find that I am given gifts, in return for these trinkets of mine, of a radiance that I neither have deserved nor desired.

It would be most refreshing to see "dating" in Indian student life; but it must be in this ethos of freedom. If dating were to serve its proper function as both an opportunity for companionship and end in itself during student days, and as a helpful introduction to "living together" in society, it should be oriented to life in general.

This purposive orientation is singularly lacking in a fatalistic system. Nor does the Dialectical Materialism of history offer it. The Self is a most cherished possession of the individual. To tell him that this Self attains its consummation in losing itself in the Ultimate, or that it achieves its fulfillment even as cannon fodder for a machine gun, be it the machine gun of dialectics or of history, is of poor comfort. Life has more in it and more to it than being a mere means to impersonal ends of *Nirvana* or Classless Society.

Further, the purposiveness has to be meaningful not only to the individual but also to the society. Human history has to be something more than endless repetition of a tale told by an idiot, full of sound and fury, signifying nothing. The grindings of the dialectic machine does not offer any creative certainty either. For instance, why the process of opposites producing synthesis should come to an automatic stop when the dictatorship of the proletariat comes to pass, is an open question. Again, why should the state "wither away?" Voluntary resignation is something alien to the very concept of communism, for, if the revolution of the proletariat is coming anyway, why fight it; and how likely does it seem that the instrument of unceasing aggression will suddenly throw up its arms and give up the ghost? That would make the Communist attack on the State look silly, would it not?

The purposiveness that is indispensable to both the individual's and the human society's lives ought to have some kind of creativity about it. Otherwise, life would not have any meaning to it. Losing oneself in an infinite, unchartered sea of the Absolute does not mark creativity, as much as it does some sort of annihilation. Classless society is admittedly the product of a kind of creativity; but then what? As in fairy tales, do "they live happily ever after?" It is hardly plausible. Power, for one thing, can corrupt in the days of a classless society just as in the days of Lord Acton; and absolute power could corrupt absolutely. Again, there can be ensured only equality of opportunity, but not of endowment. And as long as there remains intellectual inequality, there is no classlessness; Marx had to reckon with the possibility of the continuing rumblings of class war, defeating the very purpose for which the initial struggle was launched. Here again, the purposiveness is not unambiguously creative.

One more essential qualification of this purposiveness will be the certainty of it. If the end one achieves is only the knowledge that the Infinite is imponderable, then the possibility of losing oneself in the Infinite tends to be rather uncomfortable. The life-death circle is continuous; and millions of births and deaths are indispensable before the immortal soul returns to its mortal abode. How and when are widely uncertain. What about the Communistic certainty? How about the hopes of the millions who have sacrificed themselves on the altar of revolution with the hope that the Canaan they died for may one day blossom? Has it come? Or will it come? Marx thought it would be soon, maybe right after his death. Lenin probably gave it a longer time limit. What happened to the certainty that Trotsky stood for? Stalin has also gone by: but what about the ultimate victory? Is it only tarrying, or is it on its way? Or again, is it sure? Have the working men lost only their chains, or could it be that they lost something more in the process? Was it all worth it? What is the certainty? Without creative certainty, there can be no purposiveness to precious human lives, which are the creation of a wisdom transcending dialectics, worthy of joyful realization in creative freedom.

It was unfashionable in the first century when the Carpenter of Nazareth declared to the world that there was a creative purposiveness to the seemingly messy happenings of His day: the succeeding invasions of armies, internal strife and external aggression, quarrels of countries and wars of nations. He called men to be free—free from fear of the Romans, free from the bonds of slavery to dead habits and anti-creative thoughts, free from sin. Beckoning them to a glory beyond, He showed how lives could glow with the resilience of an eternal radiance. It was to no comfortable luxury to which they were called: "Come, let us also go with Him to suffer and to die." Yes, they did. One of the twelve was crucified feet upward; one was killed by an arrow just like a game animal; another was beaten to death. Yet they had the most enviable endings of their period on this earth; it was the certainty of a creative purposiveness that radiated from their crosses.

The martyrdoms of the first century are too well known to be repeated here. Walking into open death, they were victorious and jubilant. To them, life, in a sense, began after the arena.

Living martyrdoms to this hope are no old story; they are taking place today at this very moment, in the countries closed off by barriers of bamboo, iron or what not. This burning witness in lands with different degrees of religious liberty is counted as a prerogative of people; they choose deliberately to get the boot for being non-conformists. While the lions of the Roman Colosseum were open and identifiable, the consuming threats to the minds of the present-day martyrs are concealed and unidentifiably nebulous. Choice is easy when the shades are distinct; but when they are strikingly similar, and have so much in common on the surface, and continue to be so in the multitude of issues that arise from day to day and hour by hour, then the problem of keeping to the straight and narrow path of creative purposiveness becomes a battle that strains every bit of one's stamina and imagination: it is far easier to die once than to survive a living death.

Yet even as in the first century, so it is in the twentieth: men and women witness to this creative purposiveness of human history, of which theirs is a part, with a joy and freedom that is unique. Again and again, they tell us that it is not they who build this purpose for history; that even when they err and go astray, the purposiveness does not vanish. It is a certainty, a joyful certainty that they are called to be partners in a plan of which they know nothing but the Master. And they are content to play out their roles in the varying lots assigned them, content to know that they are co-workers in a plan extending both from before and beyond themselves.

This unique disposition was expressed in verse:

> It fortifies my soul to know
> That though I perish, truth is so;
> That, howsoe'er I stray and range,
> Whate'er I do, Thou dost not change.
> I steadier step when I recall
> That, if I slip, Thou dost not fall. [3]

What happens to the facts of history in the lights of this relationship?

Sure enough, the part of history composed by individual lives has a significant relationship to the Plan; other wise, the host of witnesses that have gone before, and those that are still continuing in their witness, have wasted their time and talents. However, "even if I slip, Thou dost not fall" would mean that the Plan does not hang by the single thread of an individual. How can these two views be reconciled? According to one, the symbols of my participation in the Plan are facts which go into the building of the Plan; according to the other, it would seem that all the facts are mere symbols which cannot make or mar the Plan.

> The long history of this world which God created and sustains from day to day, and for the sake of which He sent His Son, is not rendered meaningless by the coming of His Kingdom. Nor, on the other hand, is His Kingdom simply the final outcome of this world's history. There is no straight line from the labors of men to the Kingdom of God. He rejects that history of which man fancies himself to be the center, creator and lord; He accepts that history whose beginning, middle and end He Himself fixes and determines. [4]

This statement gives an inkling of the perfect compatibility of the apparently paradoxical situation of man's being an active participant in God's Plan, His Kingdom, and simultaneously God being the molder and maker of the Plan. The Kingdom of God is, like salvation, an outright gift. The Apostle Paul expressed a similar paradox—the paradox of salvation—when he wrote: "Therefore, work your own salvation with trembling, knowing that it is the Lord who worketh in you." While a gift, yet you work for it. While you work for it, you realize that it is *not* your work which molds the gift but that the gift itself is beyond all that you can either deserve or even desire. It is this meaningless meaningfulness that alone can give the correct perspective to the facts of life and of history. It is only the Truth that can make men free from philosophic inactivity and Communistic activation and set the world back in its moorings.

We spoke of a creative certainty. What is the creativity and the certainty about the Kingdom of God? Its *creativeness* lies in part in the fact that the Plan that unfolds dimly before us now, will be revealed fully later; we would then know that our labors were never thrown away. Its *certainty* is in that it is already come.

Multitudes ask themselves, "What is coming to the World? What is in front of us? What may we look forward to?"

The answer to these questions has been given to us in the Gospel. To those who ask "What is coming to the World?" We answer "His Kingdom is coming."

To those who ask "What is in front of us?" we answer "It is He, the King, who confronts us."

To those who ask "What may we look forward to?" we answer that we face not a trackless waste of unfilled time with an end that no one can dare to predict; we face our living Lord, our judge and Saviour, He who was dead and is alive for evermore, He who has come and is coming and will reign for ever and ever. [5]

So it is a Kingdom that is come and in which we are living; and it is for a Kingdom that will have its consummation in the future that we are working. What can be more certain than that which already is? What can be more creative than the transformation of an existing order into a completely new one: new in form and feature, far beyond the imagination?

Here is the new perspective that we have been looking for; the perspective which would transcend history by transmuting it, and not fail and fall with history; the perspective wherein the facts would neither be symbols, nor symbols facts, but the symbolism of the facts and the factual nature of symbols will both have their point and purpose in unfolding the infinite Plan which consummates in the gift of the Kingdom of God which is both come and coming.

What would be the practical implications of this perspective for the adjustments necessitated by the introduction of machinery in Indian life?

Poet Rabindranath Tagore, in his famous book of poems *Gitanjali,* makes a beautiful prayer:

Where the mind is without fear and the head is held high;
Where knowledge is free;
Where the world has not been broken up into fragments by narrow domestic walls;
Where words come out from the depth of truth;
Where tireless striving stretches its arms toward perfection.
Where the clear stream of reason has not lost its way into the dreary desert sand of dead habit.
Where the mind is led forward by thee into ever-widening thought and action—
Into that heaven of freedom, my Father, let my country awake.[6]

In this heaven of freedom, the exercise of the right to choose one's own mate will take its proper place. And dating will play a part in this. There will be freedom and happiness because dating, as any other social institution, derives its point and purpose from a higher goal than merely momentary relaxation. Womanhood can no longer be treated as symbolic of subservient productivity, but must play an equal, though dissimilar, role to that of men in the Kingdom of God.

The older generation again comes into their own when this new perspective orientates the lives of men and women. In fact, the organic nature of the present relationship in the family will have its fulfillment when the old folk are attended to as a spontaneous result of affection.

Individual enterprise and marriage will be healthier, again, because these are seen in the true perspective.

This is but the beginning.

The views of a people on life or living, or their manner of ordering it will not change overnight.

It will have to start with the present social unit, the family. The members of the family will first have to see the glorious freedom that is theirs. They will have to appropriate the privilege of co-workership in the Plan which is certain, creative, and which endows freedom to the participants and emancipation to the personalities involved.

Does it mean that all machinery will have to wait till the people are made free to take to it? This could never be; for one thing, freedom is a dynamic concept and not a static state of sublime inactivity; and for another, 400 million people will take quite a while before they appropriate the same sense of freedom.

This would mean that the vital point in Indian economic development would be to provide this orientation to the entire program. This vision of enabling the people to be free to choose their freedom, is one without which all plans would perish; because it is the human material which, in the final analysis, will have to cope with the changes in the inanimate surroundings, be it in the use of soap to wash or machines to mow; and it is the human material which will have the choice of making freedom a pretense for licentiousness or making it a sweet fragrant offering, acceptable for the Highest Purposes.

Where there is no vision, the people perish.

CHAPTER TEN

"QUICK MARCH"

The need for a positive philosophy of life—fumblings in agriculture—fumblings in industry—the scope of regional planning.

SHANKAR IS AN INDIAN CARTOONIST. His journal is perhaps the pioneer attempt at providing a medium through which the nation may laugh at itself. Among the early cartoons on Prime Minister Nehru is one with the caption: "The Missing Word."

Nehru is seen shouting "Quick March." Indians march in frantic hurry—some to the left, some to the right, some backward, some forward, and others are lost in a frenzy of marching all around. Everyone is marching vigorously, but they do not seem to get anywhere.

The ensuing confusion, arising out of good intentions being wasted by poor directives, is epitomized in the caption: "The Missing Word." When the command "Quick March" is given to an army, it is always told how to conduct its marching operation: forward, by the left, by the right, etc. Because the vital word is missing in the command given to the people of India, they waste their energy in insufficient and, in part, even undirected activity.

This directive can never be a negative one in the form of avowed opposition to communism. It may be good politics to oppose Communists, but it is not the best method of socio-economic development to be obliged to aim national goals for mere opposition to any particular philosophy of living.

Socialism is voiced as the pattern for Indian society. But there has been very little effort expended on formulating the implications of different brands of socialism and their relevance to the Indian situation. Certainly, rigorous thinking on vital issues of a nation's way of living can ill-afford to be left to the whimsical fancies of self-appointed social reformers. It must be subjected to the most thorough examination by competent social scientists, and then presented to the people of the land for wide and vigorous appraisal in the press and in open meetings before it is accepted as the pattern for the country. As long as this is not done, the current practice of every minister airing his own brand of "ism" can only lead to a decreasing respect for their particular views, and increasing general confusion.

Even the adaptation of socialism would not serve to meet the challenge of the Indian situation. As has been pointed out in the preceding chapters, it is a positive, concrete and creative philosophy of action that is called for by the people. This philosophy of action *would* say, "by the right, or by the left" to the development policies of the country, be they pertaining to agriculture or industry, to production or distribution.

Where there is no vision, the plans perish. The plans should be realistic; they should also be lofty, working out practices stemming from principles that are basic to the life of the nation.

The rich heritage of the people should be adequately protected. By providing conditions conducive to the progressive discovery and appropriation of these values, the program of socio-economic development would serve to entrench the democratic foundations of life as the means of tireless striving towards individual fulfillment in society.

But man lives also by bread; and if a beggar is given a vote, he would be obliged to sell it to the first man who gives him bread.

The major alternative promise of bread comes from Communist quarters. In order to demonstrate the ability of non-violent methods to provide lasting solutions to pressing problems, a new philosophy of action should be continually evolving, providing the proper orientation to the periodic programs of development, and incorrect and slovenly thinking habits that weaken existing programs should be immediately spotted and remedied.

Perhaps a striking illustration of unrigorous thinking in agriculture is provided by the word-of-mouth report concerning the ill-conceived and ill-fated attempt to clear sub-Himalayan forests. Somebody thought it a good idea to clear the forests at the foot of the great mountain range and, apparently without the least forethought as to the possible consequences of deforestation, went ahead with the program. It is said that in the first year, about 50,000 acres were cleared, and nearly a quarter million acres in the second. When it was seen that the peasants would not go to cultivate the new lands, panic started. All kinds of people were sought to cultivate the land; ex-army men were given special privileges and earlier discharges if only they would go and settle down in the new lands. With great difficulty, about half of these lands were brought under unwilling cultivation. The first year of cultivation proceeded without serious mishaps; but then came the floods, which, in the absence of the forest to stop the rainfall, swept the cleared areas, carrying away the entire crops. The project, which involved substantial investment in men and machinery, was dropped like a hot potato, and the scandal had to be hushed up.

This is no isolated incident. Its citation at this point is not intended as much an indictment of inefficiency, as an illustration of unseemly haste in precipitating immediate results without adequate regard to the future.

Julian Huxley made the following observations in the course of an interview just before he left India in April, 1954:

You are up against a spread of population so great that pressure on the land grows to such an extent that even unsuitable land is pressed into cultivation and deforestation is increased. There is the deplorable example of a Government-established fertilizer factory that works on wood fuel and, in order to feed it, trees throughout the neighborhood are being cut down. Thus, in order to produce artificial fertilizers, trees are being destroyed and the land robbed of its natural fertilizers.

It is shocking to learn that the progress of deforestation since Independence has been much faster than ever before in the history of the country.

The lack of Government control is most regrettable. Enormous benefits would accrue if only the results of the good work done by the Forest Research Institute were applied. The two problems need to be tackled together: the pressure of population on the soil and the imperative necessity to check deforestation and to increase afforestation instead. [1]

Another kind of inadequately rigorous thinking in matters of planning is evidenced in the numerous self-sufficiency drives. Jute, tea, and cotton textiles are responsible for nearly 80 per cent of India's earnings of foreign currency. It is most desirable that India have a relative sufficiency in the supplies of the respective raw materials of these semi-manufacturing and manufacturing industries. So far, so good.

The partition of the country almost necessitated the achievement of self-sufficiency in raw jute. In less than six years, near-self-sufficiency was achieved in the interests of survival as a jute manufacturers exporting country. Cotton could not be neglected in view of the potential markets in South East Asia: so there was a "Grow More Cotton" campaign. How about tea? That was a pretty good foreign exchange earner too. So let more of it be grown. Now, this is more or less what happened in the first few years. The plethora of "Grow More" Campaigns was the result of targets set without proper integration. Because the land area was not as unlimited as the demands of simultaneous self-sufficiency targets, there arose the problem of settling priorities. The fact that the priorities had to be fixed *after* the Plan was under way is a poor compliment to the organization of the Plan. Should food first be grown to the point of self-sufficiency? Or jute? Or cotton? Or something else? For, common sense dictates that you cannot have it all at once on the same land area: a simple truth, yet often overlooked.

Another instance of imbalance in timing and technique is apparent in the hasty attempt to institutionalize machinery on the farm. Increase production by all means, but does this mean that the bulldozers should run like mad all over the country and that it would herald in the blessed agricultural revolution? The detailed implications of this have been almost totally overlooked: the integration of a plan comes in where the likes and the dislikes of the people are accorded fair consideration, where the use of machinery is an indigenous move, not thrust upon unwilling peasants in a steam-rolling process.

This steam-rolling attitude is not confined to lapses in forethought about the impact on long-established ways of living in formulating long-term plans alone. The short-term implementations also reflect somewhat unseemly haste.

There are probably several ways to get villagers to take action to improve themselves. . . . One is based upon the authority of some person or organization to punish the villagers if they fail to take the desired action . . . One of the most commonly stated advantages for the authority method sounds something like this, "Well it gets the job done, doesn't it?" The *Gram Sevak* (rural development assistant) distributed his ploughs and the development officer got the smokeless *chulas* (ovens) built.

A follow-up on these two cases revealed that several months later many of the improved ploughs distributed in this manner were lying unused in the cultivators' houses. . . . (As to the *chulas*) out of the whole village, I found one that was being used for cooking and one that was being used as a shelf for storing unused household articles.[2]

This weakness for immediate results has not infrequently led to long-term damages. Thanks to the authority-centered operation reform:

> All the cultivators who had been "persuaded" to buy ploughs by this method were disgruntled and convinced of two things. All *Gram Sevaks* were out to cheat them and all steel ploughs were no good. This closed the subject of *Gram Sevaks* and steel ploughs for these cultivators for years to come.[3]

These setbacks, experienced in the well-meant but ill-conceived efforts of Community Development Projects, underscore the necessity for wider horizons in agricultural planning. It cannot be gainsaid that reliable statistics are indispensable for deciding upon the optimum levels of output to be aimed at the methods to arrive at the targets, and the accompanying considerations of techniques, impact on the social structure, etc

It is an uncomfortable truth that agricultural statistics are among the least reliable of all available figures. When 400 million people have their food supply hanging by a few figures and these figures are far from reliable, it gives rise to a rather insecure feeling. As a matter of fact, the largest statistical organization in the country was called upon in 1951 to defend certain crop estimates that this organization had made. According to the crop forecasts, made on the basis of an agricultural survey that the organization conducted, Bihar was a surplus State. However, it turned out that during the same period when the State was supposedly having surplus stocks of food they were actually experiencing famine conditions. The statistical organization could probably answer that all that they were concerned with was the estimate of production; they had nothing to do with, or could do nothing against, maldistribution which gave rise to famine conditions. However, the fact that the organization was summoned before the court of justice to explain famine conditions reflects the importance of the crop estimates.

Indian agricultural statistics today remain essentially the same as they were in their earliest origins—a by-product of official interest in the collection of revenue. The basic unit is the village *patwari* (headman), who, among the manifold duties of sizing up land taxes, collecting them, warning default-ers or causing action to be taken on them, running a full house-hold, keeping local political factions in line, also has to cast the wizard's wise eye of discernment to make a forecast of how much food might be expected. What he is expected to do in this minor, routine job is; (a) make *ad hoc* decisions about what *is* the "normal yield" of a field; (b) measure with his mental eye the absolute potential of the season's crop by the sparse blades that are visible; (c) express this latter, not as a per cent, but on a scale divided into sixteenths; (d) give explanations for significant deviations from the previous esti-mates. Now, he has to send in four crop estimates every season —when the crops are first sown, fully sown, half grown, and then the "final" forecast when the harvest is near. There also will have to be another "revised" estimate, based on the actual harvest.

Being quite a thankless job, it is small wonder that the *patwari* treats the business of agricultural estimates with the casualness of the moment. For one thing, he cannot see much point in it; for another, he does not have the initiative in the matter because it is thrown in his lap as one of many trades of which he is supposed to be master, and for which he actually neither has the ability nor the desire.

It is a pity that even when the crop estimates have been undertaken by state departments and academic institutions this fundamental weakness is allowed to persist. Very fine refine-ments of assessing the standard error and the limits of variance are progressively perfected; stratified sampling and other techniques are used to reduce to a minimum the element of bias; calculating machines which can handle millions of figures are put to work to tabulate and process the date. However, the source of primary data still remains as weak as it was in the earliest days, with the exception that the *patwari* has given place to someone who is just as equally burdened and uninterested in the whole operation. The time needed to travel from one sample point to another in an agricultural survey is calculated precisely; the sample points themselves are investigated by two different surveyors at different times under the "interpenetrating sample points" arrangement. But even though there is an attempt made to check errors, it is also known that the two surveyors of the same plot, each one of whom is theoretically unaware of the other surveyor assigned to the same plot, not infrequently manage to compare notes before turning in the results in order to escape the necessity of explaining any discrepancies between the two reports.

This illustrates two basic defects of the current approach to agricultural development. The first one is that the most vital sources of information are allowed to be the weakest. The men in the field are the lowest paid in the entire hierarchy of statistical workers engaged in crop estimates. They have to run from plot to plot and repeat the gymnastics of first deciding on an average crop, then estimating the crop from the first blades and finally expressing the estimates in difficult fractions. For this high statistical skill, nothing more than bare literacy is supposed to be adequate. And what is obtained is the least paid, least skilled technician possible, who could not care less for anything than the duty of figuring out the future crop. There is neither ability, aptitude nor incentive involved in the work. How could the figures so obtained be anything other than what they are today—a sheer gamble, and a poor one at that, on the credulity of man!

On the other hand, technicians who have plodded through

weary days of dreary theoretical gymnastics in statistics for a full two or three years, who eagerly look forward to getting down to doing something constructive after the penury of the academic years, are sadly disillusioned and frustrated when most of them are doomed to the thankless task of the eternal comparison of figures for accuracy. They are put in those places because the primary data gathering is too "low-brow" for the scholars from the universities. If any interest at all can be cultivated, it would be in those students; and no sooner do they offer their services than they are turned lose on the dull, dreary desert of monotonous figure comparison. Even the potential wings of interest in statistics are clipped, crudely and callously, in their earliest birth struggles.

To add to the lopsidedness of the arrangement checks and counterchecks are placed on the *estimators*, rather than on the estimates. This gives rise to a second basic defect. You starve a man, intellectually, emotionally and financially. You load him with the sacred duty of searching tirelessly for the truth. Knowing the absurdity of your own proposition, you set watch over the weary path that he is supposed to trek cheerfully for the sake of the safety of his nation's food estimates. After driving him so systematically from despair to frustration and from frustration to dejection, you still demand sterling honesty. The Pharisees in the first century could not have appeared much worse in their fanaticism. They loaded men's backs to breaking with ramifications of the Commandments, and beat them black and blue with the sordid certainty of eternal hell when men sunk under the weight of the Commandments. They not only sank under the weight, but before they sank, they invented means of successfully evading some of the Commandments by taking them literally and not seriously. The Pharisee –like zeal for moral righteousness, while disregarding the human element thus produced not only flagrant violations but also the persistent *impulse* to violation. Similarly, in the estimates of agricultural statistics, the present system not only creates violations of the duty to be conscientious in reporting estimates and making them, but also continuously contributes to the creation of an *impulse toward dishonesty*. It is thus twice cursed: it curseth him that estimates and him that uses the estimates; it corrupts both the estimator and the estimate, and, worse than that, it produces men who are driven to dishonesty to their own and the nation's peril.

Obviously, the cure lies in tackling the basic cause. The job of agricultural estimates should no longer be left as an unwanted by-product of overburdened underdogs. It should be placed squarely on the shoulders of those who are qualified to do it. However, it should not be overlooked that the raw graduates may fare pretty poorly in their early attempts, not having had much chance to see how the crops grow and how they look and what an "eye estimate" calls for. But it will be worth it; for one thing, the students will have an opportunity to be less frustrated; for another, and this is important, they would not be bothered about making their estimates conform to the earlier ones, because they could devote more time to explanations of why the discrepancies arise than the *patwari* who is too care-worn or the surveyor who is chased from pillar to post.

And they must be paid handsomely for this very important and crucial job. It might be interesting to compare the status of another civil servant, the policeman, in England and in India. Ultimately, being the lowest symbol of law and public order, he is the one on whom law and public order rests; yet in India, it still remains by and large, the poorest of vocations, the lone symbol of law also being a low symbol of social status. Result: the police becomes a by-word for corruption. While in the foreground the distinguished judges in impressive headgears strain to see that no one is punished unjustly, in the background the frustrated constables batter the bodies of potential criminals, not to evoke the truth, but to elicit obligatory contributions to their own personal budgets. In England it is a respectable job to be a policeman. He is well-paid, well-dressed, and he has his place in society. His counterpart in India enjoys the reverse of these privileges, and it cannot be gainsaid that the progress of justice in India will depend, not so much on the judiciary, but on an uplifting of the police constabulary, because the perfection of the former alone would remain a lopsided development, tipping the scales in favor of the executive arm of the law, and taking back all that the judicial arm seeks to endow to the public life.

Therefore, one of the very early steps to be taken to make the Five Year Plan relevant to the objectives it stands for, including the improvement of agriculture, is to renovate *ab initio* the agricultural statistics of the country. Pertinent to this would be the proper remuneration of really skilled workmen to provide the basic figures on which the whole edifice of national food statistics are built.

So also, in order to save efficiency from expediency, and lasting benefit from the encroachment of immediate ends, the very basis of agricultural development should be rethought and priorities established in the light of a wide perspective.

An assessment of India's Industrial growth records the following:

In less than nine years of independence India has demonstrated remarkable ingenuity and enterprise in attempting to to provide the first measures of economic decency to its 372 million people. Thanks to a dynamic Five Year Plan (1951–56) agricultural production has increased 15 per cent. By placing 12 million more acres under irrigation the nation has become self-sufficient in food grains for the first time in this century. Transportation, communications, and social services have improved at a pace never before witnessed. But most outstanding among India's achievements has been a *43 per cent increase in industrial production.*

Iron and steel, engineering, cement, chemicals, textiles, and agricultural processing all have expanded rapidly, and a wide variety of products never before manufactured are now available. Both the national and state governments, in addition to private capital, have participated actively in this growth. Several billion dollars have been spent to carry out a policy of nationalization and control where essential to ensure production. Even though many types of manufacturing must now be protected to compete with imports, the governmental program has emphasized the creation of at least a nucleus of diversified industries whose products eventually can replace costly imports.[4] (Italics supplied)

This kind reference to the state of Indian industry and agriculture covers more than what it discloses. When it is said that "the nation has become self-sufficient in food grains for the first time in this century," it is not made clear that this self-sufficiency relates only to cereal production which, while a commendable gain in itself, does not justify the waste in deforestation, soil erosion, and impoverishment of the resources of the land on a long-term basis. Nor does the reference indicate the unreliable agricultural statistics on which the 15 per cent increase is based. Also omitted are the ill-conceived conflicting priorities that have sprung up in the name of self-sufficiency.

Similarly, the "43 per cent increase in industrial production" hides woeful stories of feeble measures and wrong steps taken to mobilize the country's industrial potential. Inefficiency in the iron and steel industry resulted in an international team's inspection of the industry at the request of the Government of India. Old types of machinery still used in the country's most important foreign exchange earning industries have adversely effected the status and prospects in an increasingly competitive world market.

Perhaps the worst feature of industrial planning is the concentration of industries in the northern, central, and western parts of India, almost to the exclusion of the south. While the north does have mineral deposits and other industrial materials the south contributes a good share of the manpower necessary to these industries.

Even when the requisite raw materials are available, the industries have not been located in the place of origin of these same materials. Thorium is a mineral which is found almost entirely in Travancore (now part of Kerala State) in the south. Yet the thorium plant was located not in the south but in the northwest, nearly 1,200 miles away from Travancore.

The reason for shifting the site of the industry from Travancore was reported to be the fear of letting atomic materials fall into the hands of communists.

It would appear that this policy would play the people into the hands of the communists more than anything that the communist party itself would be able to do. Imagine millions of highly qualified, educated unemployed who cannot find a job in Travancore. There is the possibility of the thorium factory providing employment to some of them. More than the employment actually provided, the factory becomes a symbol of improving prospects of employment. Suddenly, without ceremony, the plant is to be located near far-away Bombay. It does not need the imagination of the communists to whip up political discontent on the basis of this particular location of industry alone. And the proposed location is in the proximity of an already highly crowded industrial area.

The targets of the second five year plan do not seem to attempt at correcting this lopsidedness either.

Steel is very much on India's mind. Right now Russians, Americans, Germans, and Britons are helping India build new plants or are drawing up new plans for them.
(Not one of the new plants are to be located in south India)

Two oil refineries, Standard Vacuum and Burma Shell, have gone into production and Caltex is building another. They represent an investment totaling $106,000,000, the largest foreign investments in independent India.

(Not one of the refineries are located in south India)

The goals for the second five-year plan, to start in April of this year, (1956) are ambitious. India hopes to produce 5,000,000 tons of steel; the first plan target was 1,300,000. India hopes to produce 10,000,000 tons of cement; the first plan target was 4,600,000. (A small fraction of cement production will be carried out in south India) India hopes to produce 60,000,000 tons of coal; the first plan target was 37,000,000 (No fraction of coal production is carried out in south India). [5] (Parenthetical comments supplied)

This lopsidedness can be permitted to persist only at great peril to India's democratic way of life.

If the battle for democracy loses its fight in the south, it will not be because of ignorance or poverty, but more than either of these, it will be due to ill-conceived industrial location which does not alleviate the problem of the educated unemployed.

If some brother or sister has no clothes and has not food enough for a day, and one of you says to them, "Goodbye, keep warm and have plenty to eat" without giving them the necessaries of life, what good does it do? [6]

An unindustrialized south is an open avenue to communism. In the fertile minds of young, educated Indians, who are anxious to do something for their country, seeds of discontent are repeatedly cast by the disappointing response from the few sources of employment. Frustrated idealism, enlightened education, dammed efficiency—the Communists have use of them.

The educated unemployed are like a traveler in the dark. Religion has been for ages the one source of light that the people looked to for guidance. At the hour of despondency instinct urges him to knock at the door of the church or of the temple. Therefore, at the midnight of his life, when nobody else watches, he goes to the church or the temple and knocks.

It is the knock of a traveler in the night who has seen the

eternal steeple casting its impressive imprint even in the dark.
Did the traveler come to it, searching for figs out of season?
Did the knock wake up those within or do they never hear
the knock? If they ever wake up, they would find that they
have nothing to set before the traveler. They will have to go
and beg of their Friend to lend them a few loaves to set before
the weary traveler, who is now an accepted guest. Does the
church or the temple wake up to open the door, to accept the
traveler, only to be confronted with its own impoverishment
and to beg of its Master Who alone can lend some loaves?
Some of the worship centers are thus allowing themselves to
be led by the Spirit into the wilderness of involvement with
the human problems of want; but most of them still choose
to go to the Cross via some other method.

What about the traveler in the dark? He knocks and waits.
If the door does not open, if the only light he has been used
to all the days of his life fails him, what can he do in the
pitch darkness that surrounds him? Go on, he must.

The traveler in the dark sees little fireflies. To him, faced
with the alternative of pitch darkness, even those shimmering
lights are a welcome relief. Even as a drowning man clutches
at a piece of straw, he grabs at the opportunity to follow the
shimmering fly which gives him the lingering hope of light.

It is the traveler who could not see the light that he came
in search of who goes out stumbling in search of lesser lights.
This traveler wanted to live and not merely survive; he wanted
to achieve something constructive, not being content with complacency. He also wanted sustenance. But even if he did not
have any of these, did he at least get an encouraging answer:
friendly call? Ashamed of its inadequacy, but unwilling to
beg for loaves that it may set before its midnight guest, the
worship center tries in vain to pass on apologies of inaction.
Social justice? Equality of opportuity? Shshsh . . . Let us go
to church on Sundays and it will be alright. Do not breathe
these strange slogans which are on the Red Flag . . .

The traveler wants action. And the Communist Party offers it. The traveler wants food. And the Communist Party promises it, if only the traveler would join hands with them to knock off a few who have too much food. Where the church is not the church, there the Communist Party steps in to recruit able and willing hands with the promise of an ideal to fight for, and something to die for.

Impression minus expression equals depression. The traveler therefore chooses either expression or depression. The church, as long as it is apologetic, can counsel only depression, because it advises no program of action; the Communist Party urges expression. Possibly, it also leads to depression; but, like the man who shouted "so far so good" as he passed every floor in his fall from the top of the thirty-floor building, those travelers riding on the crest of expression would be content to leave the question of oncoming depression alone.

Lopsided location of industry is responsible for part of this depression; that part is curable, the situation is remediable.

The Government can set about attacking this problem by keeping in mind the need for employment of the 175 million inhabitants of the southern part of this sub-continent as the consideration of location of new industrial units come up. This is a problem involving co-operative action on the part of the central and state governments. For instance, when considering the location of the next oil refinery, it might be worthwhile to think of Vizag as a possible site. Vizag is the only natural harbor of Southern India on the eastern coast. In refining oil the crude material is brought from Assam. Even if this were to incur a higher cost of transportation than say to a refinery in Bombay, the extra cost would be worth the while of the Government because Vizag so badly needs some area of endeavor for her numerous unemployed. Bombay may have the additional advantage of having two other refineries in the vicinity, which would help in obtaining skilled labor more easily. Here again, the advantage of employing the unemployed would outweigh the disadvantage of the absence of skilled labor.

The lopsided arrangement of industrial location, internally, has its unpleasant parallels in developmental efforts externally that could be far more significantly effective. Two primary consequences of this state of affairs are felt in India's export trade and in international investments in India.

Inadequate considerations of industry's long-term future, as against trade's short-term gains, were reflected in the Government's spiralling export duty imposed on jute.

Export duty on jute manufactures was doubled from $150 to $300 per ton of *hessian* (manufactured jute) between October and November, 1950, and then it was cut down first to $150 in February, 1952, and then to $55 in less than three months. What does this mean to the trade? The exporters in India enter into contracts with the importers abroad on the basis of say $150 export duty, and by the time their consignment is due to be shipped, the rate goes up to say $200; they alter their agreements in the light of the changed circumstances, and, *voilà*, the shipload arrives in New York with the duty having risen to $300. Whether the exporter bears the duty or passes it on to the importer, it is the trade of the nation which suffers. By the time the government reversed the process and slashed the duty, the damage was already done.

Mineral exporters had a similar experience. Manganese was a rising foreign exchange earner. Different companies are engaged in the trade, some big, some small. This story is that of the big manufacturer. The customs make *ad hoc* rates of export duty, depending on the market quotations. The small firm may sell a lot at a price higher than the rest of them. And the export duty is raised because the highest selling price is taken into account and not the average; with the result that the big sellers lose the good will of their big buyers. But the story is not over. The buyer has to pay duty on the basis of the mineral content of the ore that the seller is exporting. And the determination of this mineral content hangs upon the arbitrariness of the low-paid petty officer at the customs who can generally claim innocence of any knowledge of mineralogy. His arbitrariness, however, being final, continually contributes to the ire of the buyer who finds that he he has to pay an altogether different amount than the one he was prepared to pay at the time of the receipt of the advice of the despatches.

Admittedly, while these complaints of the exporters would naturally be colored, it is apparent that this does reflect a sad state of weak motivations and wrong measurements based on a vaguely (if at all) defined system.

The vagueness arises out of uncertainty as to whether or not a flourishing export trade is the goose that lays the golden eggs of foreign exchange. The treatment of the goose depends on the attitude towards the eggs it lays. If killed early, the loss may be both the eggs and the goose.

While the efforts at capturing the cream of the profits of the jute exports were afoot, a large lapse developed at the production end. India, not being self-sufficient in raw jute, looked to Pakistan for the supply of the indispensable raw material for this prospering export industry. But Pakistan chose not to allow the Indian exporting industry to make all the advances it desired to make in the foreign markets. During the Indo-Pakistani trade deadlock in 1950, Australian importers of Indian gunnybags lost patience awaiting the arrival of the precious packing material for their largest crop, wheat. They could ill-afford to gamble the entire proceeds from their crop on the uncertain supplies of packing materials from India. Consequently, Australia went ahead with the construction of bulk-handling systems which could do without gunnybags. The heavy investments in bulk-handling machinery, once made, must then be used over the years before the investment pays its way. Thus India sustained considerable damage in her Australian market for jute goods.

Was this avoidable? Under the safety of a post-mortem

examination, one may answer in the affirmative. The method of approach would be one of entering into an understanding with Pakistan so that India could assure Australia of supplies of gunnybags. In order to bring this about, it may have been necessary to impress upon Pakistan the fact that the loss of the Australian market for India would mean a proportionate loss to Pakistan also; because if Australia does not buy Indian gunnybags, India would not want Pakistan's raw jute, and raw jute is East Pakistan's mainstay of economic life.

This brings up the possibility of the regional approach.

The region would be the relevant economic unit for the production and/or distribution of any one commodity or groups of commodities in question. For instance, the jute region would be composed of India and Pakistan on the production end. Australia, the United States, Great Britain, Cuba and Argentina would comprise the region from the distribution end of jute.

Similar regional classifications can be worked out for tea: India, Pakistan and Ceylon as the production region; Great Britain and the United States on the distribution end. Cotton textiles production and consumption also permit of the formation of regions: India on the production, and the Middle East on the distribution end.

In all the three cases, it can be shown that there are means of forming coalitions among the producers to best protect their interests. Recently it has become possible to work out the exact details of these potential coalitions. *The Theory of Games and Economic Behaviour* [7] is the pioneering work in this field.

The Theory of Games is a complex mathematical tool, carefully developed over sixteen years of intense research by the late mathematician John Von Neumann of the Institute of Advanced Study at Princeton.

If a fairly crude presentation of the technique of the Game Theory be attempted, it might be started with a game in which there are just two persons. One person's gain is the other's loss and the net result of the game is zero. As soon as there are three persons the whole pattern is changed; it is no longer the simple process of one man gaining what the other loses. There arises the possibility that two of them might combine against the third. It is to the credit of the Game Theory that this entirely revolutionary conceptual emphasis was introduced into economic discussion. The combination of any two against a third is again based on the proposition that the gain from the combination is greater than that from the individual plays. As the number increases, the number of possible alternatives and coalitions increase also; and the calculations entering into the assessment of gains and losses with and without combinations also become increasingly complex.

The relevant calculations in the case of the jute "game" would, for instance, include the compensation of Pakistan for not manufacturing jute and letting India do the whole manufacturing. There is the question as to how much raw jute India and Pakistan each should be producing in order to ensure the optimum supply of manufactures. This will have to outweigh the advantage of the two countries severally competing with each other for world markets. There are considerations both of the quantity and price, and the delicate questions of compensations involved: of price for quantity and vice versa. These are some of the more obvious calculations that enter into any quantitative appraisal of the nature and extent of the possible coalitions.

The general nature of the co-operative ways of obtaining better results would indicate the need for some kind of planned development. It may be that Burma and Ceylon would agree not to produce any cloth of their own for three years to come; or better still, whether they do or not, they might agree to buy an agreed amount of cotton textiles from India. In the case of jute, India may agree to purchase annually a stipulated amount of raw jute from Pakistan for a few years. Ceylon may agree to produce not more than say one-third the amount of India's tea crop for another five years.

Involved in all this hypothetical planned development is the arrangement to keep in step. The quantities of produce will have to be decided on a regional basis, taking into account the factors entering into consumption, e.g., past demand, present and future income, and foreseeable changes in social habits and prestige values. The voluntary nature of the agreement should lend it the necessary binding strength.

The discussion so far has tacitly assumed that it was only the interests of the producers that had to be taken into consideration. National economic policies are rarely altruistic in intent, and hence this would be a justifiable assumption. However, it will be worthwhile to inquire if the way to gain by one country is only through the loss of another. While the element of loss is inevitable, it may be questioned as to whether or not there is an alternative to robbing one another. This query is posed in a new perspective—namely, that which includes in its scope, not only the producing countries, but also the consuming nations.

Economic propositions are built on the assumption of "rational behavior." The Theory of Games, as an economic tool similar to calculus as a mathematical tool, should be based on some assumption or other; the theory assumes rationality on the part of the participants of the economic game: "The aim of all participants in the social economy, consumers as well as entrepreneurs, is assumed to be money or a single monetary commodity; and further this is supposed to be identical with utility." [8] *Given this hypothesis,* the theory states that certain consequences follow; but the theory does not thereby make any claim to the relevance of the theory to economic phenomena until it proves that economic phenomena are identical with the game situations. The foregoing discussion of the formation of coalitions in the jute, tea and textiles "games"

only says that *if* these three are game situations, *then* the way
to handle the situation is indicated by the Theory of Games
to be such and such.[9]

In this context, the mention of a new perspective calls for
a somewhat radical alteration of the nature of "rational behavior." If A's gain is *not* B's loss, then the sum is no longer
zero as the positive value of A no longer directly cancels the
negative value of B. If the gain to one is not considered to
be exactly the loss of another, it would imply that the two
do not go by the arithmetic of the situation, but rather by
some other standard. The aim then is not to gain as much
as possible, but so to gain that the loss involved may be compensated for by some *common* advantage. In other words, the
two opposing players, A and B, look to their collective as well
as their individual gain.

Can international goodwill be reaped from enlightened self-
interest? Christian thinking in 1953 has the following to say
on the matter:

> Prudential motivation is morally inconsistent with selfless
> dedication, but because of mixed human nature, it seems that
> a dual practical objective, in part spiritual and selfless, in
> part practical and prudential, only can improve our human
> lot here and now, and promote a closer approximation to the
> Kingdom of God on earth. [10]

The old saying, "Poverty anywhere is a threat to prosperity
everywhere," was quoted early in Chapter Two. The relationship between the validity of the law of love and the reality
of the law of self-love, is a concept germane to Christian freedom in the context of poverty and prosperity. It does not seem
to be too clear that "in part spiritual and selfless, in part practical and prudential" is the Christian description of the objective of day-to-day living.

Christianity never talks of selflessness. That is a Hindu
concept pertaining to *Nirvana* which is a state where the self

is lost in the Ultimate. In His demands of His disciples, Christ never asked them to be selfless. The most materialistic religion, Christianity, has a unique place for man's personality. His self is not lost, but is fulfilled. What Christ demands of His disciples is not selflessness, but unselfishness. Therefore, one is forced to reject outright any suggestion that the Christian objective is selflessness.

Christ is too demanding ("Be ye perfect, even as your Heavenly Father is perfect") to settle for anything other than the highest as an objective for His disciples. He did not merely say "Be ye perfect," but He also promised the gift of the Holy Ghost to those who desired to be perfect. It is certain that He did not mean to say that a double-standard is the only feasible means of getting anything done, i.e., "Trust in God and ('but' might be more appropriate) keep your powder dry." In other words, the Christian objective can be nothing less than the highest, and a dual objective "in part spiritual and selfless, in part practical and prudential" does not make the grade.

The assertion that such a double standard "can promote a closer approximation to the Kingdom of God on earth" is self-contradictory. In a Kingdom of Love, anything other than Love, with a capital "L," is alien matter, and therefore will stand rejected. Closer approximation to the Kingdom comes from a closer acceptance of the Kingship of the King; and when men and women accept Jesus Christ as Lord and Saviour, what results is *not* a dual objective, but a singular purpose: to live as Christ. When nations accept the Lordship of Christ over history they can ill-afford to make offerings of mixed objectives to the King: they would find that were the whole realm of nature theirs, that too would be a present far too small, for Love, the law of the Kingdom of God, demands their ambitions, their economy, their politics, and pervades the innermost recesses of their counsels.

What are the contemporary results of the Christian accent on international economics? If this would mean that the sellers have to look also to the interests of the buyers, and vice versa, how could India and Pakistan combine against Australia and America to boost prices of jute? Again, how could India and Ceylon exercise their monopoly in tea production and sales to Great Britain?

One very important change that will come out of this new accent in international economics is that it will no longer be governed by the *Caveat Emptor* (buyer beware) principle because now both the buyer and the seller would be aware of each other's interests.

Would this mean a complete deadlock in economic transactions? No, this fear is rooted in the tacit assumption that man can only be selfish, and that his aim in economics is always to maximize his own advantage, as the well-known Utility Maximization Rule of economics holds. This principle also has found its way into the Theory of Games as was mentioned above.

Thus far the economic "game" has been considering only "Competitive Games." Even where coalitions came in, it was *not* out of any concern of one player for the gain of the other, but rather out of the prudential calculation that there was gain in the business. However, the technical equipment of economic analysis is necessarily a reflection of the basic philosophy of economic action. When the philosophy changes, so will the techniques necessarily change.

One of the striking features of a new orientation of this kind would be the enlargement of the concept of region. In discussing jute, for instance, the region will not merely be India and Pakistan, but will include America and Australia. It will be a new concept altogether, something like a Co-operative of Consumers and Producers. There will emerge out of the joint organizations, the rationalization and consequent avoidance of wastes now involved in non-co-operative economic action, owing to the constant guessing involved on either side as to the moves and intentions of the other party. This, however, will not uproot the beauty and joy of uncertainty and expectation. On the other hand, the uncertainties as well as expectations will be far more gainfully made, because there is an agreed demand for the commodity of which the seller is assured, and an agreed supply on which the buyer can count. This process is bound to raise the volume of trade and not in any way curtail it in the years to come.

The details of specific agreement will be dynamic; they will have to be worked out in the respective situations. However, the objectives can unmistakably be laid down. It will *not* be a dual objective, trying helplessly to ride at once on the two horses of "selflessness" and "prudence," but the singular one of *Christian mutual responsibilty* on the part of both buyers and sellers.

Perhaps the context of Christian mutual responsibility would reverse the trend seen at Simla in May, 1955.

United States hopes that the nations of Asia would get together for regional use of American economic aid are dying in Simla.

Since Monday finance experts representing thirteen Asian countries have been meeting in this north Indian mountain resort. They were called together by India to talk about how to get best use out of United States money. Special attention was to be paid to President Eisenhower's request to Congress for a separate $200,000,000 economic development fund for Asia. The United States deliberately kept its observers away from the Simla conference because Washington wanted ideas to come from Asians themselves. But the clear hope of the United States was that the experts would come up with some plans for putting the Eisenhower fund to use on a cooperative basis. But a major result of the Simla conference has been to show that *most countries of Asia are not ready for or are afraid of regional planning.* Instead of using the Eisenhower fund to promote the economic health of the region as whole, most countries at Simla just want most of the fund to be split up among the recipient nations . . . Other regional planning ideas on the Simla agenda also have been put aside. Japan's proposal that part of the President's fund be used to set up schools in Japan for training Asian technical workers has been discarded. So has the idea that the fund be used to help meet short-term dollar shortage of countries buying more than they are selling. Also reported to have been set aside was a suggestion for creating a permanent secretariat for regional planning. There was some talk, mostly from the Japanese, about expanding regional trade, but no proposals for it were adopted as of tonight. [11] (italics supplied)

This obituary notice on the regional basis of economic development was written by fear and mutual mistrust. So long as this root cause is not diagnosed and removed, development in Asia must necessarily remain at a lower level than its potential. While uncertainty, fear and distrust ride high, years of excellent co-operative endeavor are being wasted; and these wasted years, in turn, prepare the ground for further barren years. But the path to regional planning is neither easy nor smooth. Recently emancipated from the clutches of the sprawling octopus of colonialism, the Asian nations are wary of any junior edition of the same which may come in the garb of regional economic development.

What can be done to allay the suspicions of the Asian nations? Christian mutual responsibility is an objective which may guide the efforts at development on a basis broader than that of small national units. However, while this is something towards which programs of action can strive, it will never be realized, nor is meant to achieve realization. Rather, this is the perspective which would constantly challenge the interpretative powers of the nations.

Socio-economic development, whether of nations or of regions, is never written in a political vacuum.

No one, statesman or individual, can act on purely economic advice. *All statements of economic policy involve politics* and no separate economic advice or economic solution of a problem of policy is of any use until the modifications in it resulting from political factors have been worked out. [12] (italics supplied)

Therefore, statements regarding the new orientation of developmental pursuits must take due notice of political realities.

Perhaps one way of combining the new orientation of economic aspirations and political realities would be to work out in detail the alternate outcomes of action, one, within a national framework; two, within an international framework in which mutual distrust prevails; and three, within a regional framework based on mutual responsibility. The hours of research expended on carefully working out the alternate costs and returns of these plans would provide a basis, first theoretical, and later normative, for the comparative study of developmental policies. If carried on by independent research institutions, this research could combine the advantages of both private initiative and non-governmental sponsorship and nevertheless have definite influence in policy matters.

The potentials of the regional approach are bound to be explored increasingly in the years to come. Lest the exploration be wasted on drifting and costly trial-and-error experiments, the objectives should be spelled out before embarking on the efforts themselves.

PART III

Distribution Problems

CHAPTER ELEVEN

"THIRTEEN-AND-ONE-HALF CENTS PER HEAD!"

I should have stopped here; but I do not. The reason is obvious. You would have seen some important looking papers in my hand.

Martial law has been proclaimed in two districts of the country—in Alleppy and Sherthalai . . .

In order to assume direct responsibility, I am taking charge of the military as the Lieutenant General . . . (Quoted from author's memory)

THE OCCASION was the inauguration of the Agri-Horticultural Society in Trivandrum in November, 1946, by the *dewan* of the state of Travancore, Sir C. P. Ramaswamy Ayyar. He was referring to the action that he was taking as the executive head of the native state in order to put down a Communist-sponsored "revolution" in one of the northern districts. Beguiled by the slogan "13½ cents per head" (a little over ⅛ of an acre), the poor peasants thought that they had nothing to lose but their mortgages. They rose up and attempted to dispossess the land owners of their possessions. This *ad hoc* display of distributive justice grated with the law of the land; and stern measures were taken, epitomized in the *dewan's* statement, "martial law."

While misled, the uprising in Vyalar in Travancore was nevertheless a strong hint of what could come about if the vexing problem of distributive justice was not appropriately handled. The Indian Government's answer to the question of the distribution of land among the tillers of the soil took the necessarily long, but constitutionally acceptable, method of steering clear of expropriation by means of legislative enactments and compensation.

But problems of distribution, like problems of production, are never settled finally. Life and land do not permit of any final settlement. Problems have to be met head-on as and when they arise. The sure guarantee of minimal disturbance comes neither from military preparedness to settle matters of distribution, nor from the whimsical decisions of a dictator. It arises from a broad-based sense of justice which must be applied to distribution. The sanction of the broad base itself must be subject to continual review by the thinking public, and necessary changes must come through democratic processes of law and opinion, the two cherished guardians of the democratic way of life.

Such a broad-based sense of justice should spring from principles that are eternal. Justice then becomes a continual interpretation of lasting principles in contemporary situations. Thus conceived, the pitfalls of attributing finality to any particular order of the day would be somewhat guarded against. For, if distributive justice is a contemporaneous interpretation, the interpretation must of necessity unfold new shades and fresh nuances as time advances.

This wider concept of justice, of which distributive justice is only a part, will also constitute an effective framework for an answer to both Communism and complacence. As a system of thinking which claims finality, Communism will be found wanting in the scales of justice which refuse to be time-bound. As for the temptation to rest on one's laurels, howsoever attractive they may be, complacency will be discounted by a justice which urges a continuous challenge to the powers of human interpretation of superhuman verities.

The trump card of intellectual and emotional appeal that Communism offers lies in its avowed passion for establishing social justice. But its glory within a measured span of history will be dimmed when viewed against the wider canvas of history—a canvas which does not end with the theoretical heaven of the proletariat, but leaves plenty of room for the moving finger to write the aftermath of the dictatorship of the commoner. In that context, the demands of justice will be revealed to be more sweeping than those of the Communist even if he were to achieve the classless society. For, at best, the classless society is one in which the classes of *one particular day* are removed, and which by no means can claim to have ended classes for all time; at worst, it is a poor camouflage of the new classes and clashes that are bred in the wake of a bloody abolition of the existing classes.

But as Gandhiji said, "Even God does not dare to appear before a hungry man except in the form of bread." What does the concept of justice offer to the teeming millions on the land or in the factory without work or adequate employment?

This raises the question as to what *would* constitute justice in the distribution of the returns of the land? Should the land go to the tiller of the soil? Should this be done by "expropriating the expropriators?" Or is there a better way of effecting the very necessary process of better distribution of opportunities on the land? This is no academic discourse. The answer to this problem may very well make or break the bases of a just distributive system. The wolf is always at the door. In fact, the wolf of violence needs no particular grounds to stretch forth its sharp claws and feed on the sheep of incorrect measures and feeble action.

Panicky measure such as the large-scale clearance of forests and the terracing of mountain slopes, both of which are nature's guardians against soil erosion and disastrous floods, are short-sighted. Indiscriminate destruction of natural wealth is worse than a crime: it is a mistake. The requirements of justice cannot be appeased by offerings of the withered grain of hasty thought and ill-conceived action.

In order to make the distribution of the returns from the land a just one, the opportunities on land themselves will have to be the starting point. The peasants' disability of heavy indebtedness will have to be removed; and his abilities will have to be improved. Proceeding from the concept of justice, the practical implications for agricultural distribution are examined in Chapter Twelve.

India is no longer an agricultural country in the sense that agriculture represents the most important occupation. Industry has certainly come to stay; and the second five year plan (1956-1961) is an industry-oriented plan. The industrial worker has the advantage of organizational media for making his demands, although they are not always granted. The erstwhile peasant, when he takes to industry as a means of livelihood, need not necessarily be walking into the shadow of the history of class-struggles. However, if the basis for reorienting his thinking is not clearly worked out, the industrial worker will find a waiting and eager adviser to prove to him that he is but a cog in the capitalistic system of production for profit.

Can the industrial worker be persuaded to accept his rightful creative role in building his country both in the physical sense of multiplying human effort through the use of inanimate sources of power and in developing the characteristics of leadership becoming a new sector of national life?

JUSTICE—SOCIAL, ECONOMIC AND POLITICAL*

Rudiments of a proper perspective of distributive justice— righteousness exceeding that of the communists—reducing the peasant's inabilities—increasing peasant's abilities: credit facilities; group psychology to facilitate contraceptive practices; new methods of cultivation of consolidated landholdings; assuring equitable returns in the interim period; consideration of rent—the peasant waits.

N THE WINTER OF 1946, a large group of students were listening intently to a distinguished looking, tall Indian with a turban. He was inaugurating the Travancore University Union, the student center which was a novel feature in the life of the seat of the regional university. The university in India is comparable to many American universities rolled into one, because each university sets the standards for and conducts the examinations of candidates who are presented by affiliated colleges. On the basis of these exams are awarded the various academic degrees. After inaugurating the University Union, Dr. Sarvapalli Radhakrishnan, who later became the Vice-President of the Union of India, was requested to select a topic for the

* Among the aims of the Indian Constitution, the first ones listed are: "To secure to all its citizens Justice—social, economic and political."

Inter-University Debate which was to be held within a few days. True to the spirit of the democratic urge of the times, and truer still to the need for maintaining a broader vision befitting the stature of the country, he chose the topic: "Political Democracy by Itself is Futile."

After eighteen months, in August, 1947, when the present writer went to the villages near Madras, the coastal city on the south-eastern border of India, India had won her Independence—political democracy. The Indian flag was proudly hoisted in the villages. Having been accustomed to the suppressed national mood of frustrated aspirations, the fluttering flag was a refreshing sight. But the idealistic delight was mellowed considerably when the villagers pointed to the flag and asked: "There is the flag, but where is the food?"

Was freedom really won? Or had political democracy merely marked the freedom to fight want and misery? Would the hoary struggle for freedom be dwarfed and dimmed by the enormity of the struggles that were bared by the political freedom of the country? Was political democracy futile?

Evolutionary and revolutionary theories of progress are made and broken largely on the factor of distribution. Achievement of political emancipation by itself is only half the job appropriate distribution of the power and potentials so acquired constitutes the other, and perhaps somewhat more explosive, half. The very explosive nature of distribution opens up the possibilty of negating the dictum *noblesse oblige,* rank has its obligations. For discourse on the manner and method of distribution of power and potentials of a nation can be freely indulged in by any self-appointed prophet of equality who has never to fire a single shot in the battle for the winning of the power and potentials. On the other hand, those who did struggle to win those rights may tend to be too rigid in their maintenance of them. In order to effectively safeguard against either extremes of ardor without order or order without ardor, the basic orientation of distributive justice has to be carefully lai out so that the practices may always be compared with the precepts.

It was during the early days of the industrial revolution, when the compensations were under the critical eyes of a bewildered world, that the shocking effects of mal-distribution inspired Karl Marx to urge working men all over the world to unite to free themselves from their chains. Before him, the Utopian Socialists had struggled with the elements of the problems of appropriate distributive justice. Robert Owen and others attempted to tackle the problem without effecting radical changes in the existing order of society.

The Marxian conviction was that these were utopian ideas. It would be a waste of time to assume that human nature being what it is, any good would come out of the palliations of distribution; they need radical, revolutionary changes. Both Nietzsche and Marx agreed in their analyses of the premises for social change. Both were aware that history had to be changed. If the evils of lopsided distribution were to be avoided, there was only one way for Marx: the history which is the history of class struggles must be accelerated. How could this be done? Expropriate the expropriators. When history is thus changed, Marx assumed that men will be changed. In that heaven of freedom, men will be fair to one another and there will be no longer be vicious exploitation of one man by another.

The twentieth-century alternative to Marx, as reflected in contemporary Christian thinking, seeks to handle the delicate question of distributive justice and Christian charity.

> Standards of justice may be said to be (i) expressions of the law of love, insofar as the love of neighbor requires a calculation of *competitive claims* when there is more than one neighbor (ii) a practical compromise between the law of love and the law of self-love.
>
> Christian contribution is not a precise formulation of the standards of justice. It is mitigation of the severity of the

conflict which will prevent men from heedlessly seeking their own interests in the name of justice and from recklessly dominating value preferences, other than their own, as evil. If Christian piety or any other kind of piety does not yield these fruits of humility and charity, it must be consistently rejected as the "salt that has lost its savor." [1]

If one may borrow Hegelian terminology in the foregoing formulation, justice may be looked upon as the synthesis of the law of love and the law of self-love. But here is the rub. Hegelian premises pre-suppose a thesis and anti-thesis. But perfect love and self-love are *not* anti-thetical. The latter is opposed to the former in a number of instances perhaps, but it can find fulfillment only in the former. Hence, they cannot be treated as anti-one-another. By the same token it becomes necessary to find room for the operation of the latter in the framework of the wider freedom of the former. When self-love tends to seek freedom and create oppression, when it tries to achieve peace but gives rise to war; when self-love benumbs itself by its own excesses in pleasures that cloy, then *perfect* love ever holds that vision without which people perish. More than just a judge who condemns guilt, perfect love acts as a work of art. When confronted with it, everyone makes his own comments—favorable, unfavorable, indifferent. And these comments in turn reflect what is in them, aesthetics, crudity, spinelessness. The judgment was not pronounced by the piece of art; but its confrontation occasioned a revelation that was humiliating to the inadequacies of the confronted.

Therefore, any hypothesis of justice implicitly based on the anti-thesis between love and self-love is in danger of losing the perspective altogether. At the same time, it must be remembered that there is no straight line from the involvement of self-love to the elevation of perfect love. The Christian view on love and self-love will therefore be one which will take into account the fulfillment that self-love seeks to obtain by approximating itself to love as closely as possible.

In the light of this, justice takes a different turn. It derives its form and title not from a kind of practical compromise between mundane self-love and celestial perfect love, but from being the contemporary approximation to the Eternal Love which is the Law of Life.

Immediately, the problems of complacency in any social system identified with the Kingdom of God, as well as any arrogance which will identify dissimilar systems with evil, are dealt with. For, no system, however humane it might be, will be looked upon as final: "we are only useless servants, who have done but what was told." Only this perspective will lend humility and charity, simultaneously inspiring courage and confidence. Justice is then shorn of its taint of rigid blindness as something arising out of dusty lawbooks. Attention is focused upon its truly dynamic nature. And no charity has to be pleaded on the behalf of any unusual by-product of a practical compromise.

What are the implications of this dynamic concept of justice? First of all, this means that, to quote the opening sentence of the Report on the Commission on Social Questions at the Second Assembly of World Council of Churches at Evanston, "Christian Social Responsibility is grounded in the mighty acts of God." The mighty acts of God, climaxing in the gift of His Son, revealed to the world a Father who is actively concerned with the material needs of His children.

Secondly, this would mean that there will necessarily always be greater and lesser injustice. One who is concerned can ill-afford to sit by any economy in which some people have less than their share of the world's good things because others have more than their share.

The communists claim great concern over the unequal distribution of opportunity: so does the Christian. The rudiments of a proper perspective of distributive justice seem to share some elements in common with the communists. Do they differ only in name? Remember Chapter One: somebody wanted to become a communist because he was a Christian.

What then is the difference between a Christian and a Communist? Both work for the classless society: but the perspectives are different. One believes in the materialistic interpretation of history and pins hope on the dialectical process; the other believes in the immediate implications of the Lord of history being victorious now and in the end. One sees in the fight for distributive justice the necessary elimination of a whole class of people who are given a bad name and hung for the "exploitation of the masses." The other steadfastly holds that wading through the blood of brother-man is not the way to achieve justice or peace.

However, this position is by no means easy or obvious to an innumerable number of people professedly belonging to the Church. Those who are unsympathetic will attribute running with the hare and hunting with the hounds to the nonconfirmist Christians, who refuse to blame capital or labor exclusively and who seek to share the sin of both in erecting their own barriers against each other. The common people would say "What is the difference? Are you not a Communist?"

While the Church cannot identify itself with any social system, some of its members will have to bear their witness to the certainty of the Lordship of Christ over history in and through active affiliation with existing political parties. As in the Olympic games, the fire will have to be kept glowing throughout the season while different games are being played. The fire symbolizes the spirit of the game, the philosophy of man's mastery over muscles. While the different efforts to man the body are in progress, the fire still symbolizes the general theme without fear or favor. The Church is to hold the torch high—the torch which proclaims Christ as the Hope. It would have entirely diverse implications depending on the region where they are applied; and still more diverse interpretation to the people of the same region. In Germany, there are Christians who join the Democratic Party and there are those who join the Socialist Party. The Church is called upon there not to pass judgments over one or the other. It should rather shine forth so that members of its fold, whether they are running the mile or jumping the hurdles, alike be inspired in their common aim, derived from the Source of Inspiration common to both.

A third point of vital importance in the Church's inspiration in times of struggle for distributive justice is that it is the unique institution which comprises in its fold, both the "exploited" and the "exploiters" *on identical footing*. In the Church, everyone is a sinner who stands judged and saved at the Cross. The preaching of the contextual nature of Christian ethics will expose the Church to dissatisfaction from both ends; but it has got to bear this cross, and continually incarnate the Word in every situation. In many instances, the Church may be able to just keep alive a true sense of humility which would recognize that the other fellow might have something to say. There may be occasions when the Church will have to make pronouncements on present-day society. Composed of human beings, it is bound to make mistakes. When the Great Scorer comes to write against each name, He does not look to see whether you lost or won, but rather to see how you played the game. It is immaterial that mistakes are made: the relevant consideration is *how* the mistakes are made.

So, the Church is called upon to make mistakes, and to make them boldly, but with an awareness that it might be wrong at any time in its interpretation of Eternal Love to the contemporary situation.

This dynamic concept of justice provides the standard for distributive justice in economics as well as politics. It is only the freedom that comes from the call to be witnesses in the wilderness, over the tumults of unsanctified longings, in spite of disheartening situations, that can make the handling of the vehicles for distributive justice a process in fulfillment and an assurance in purposiveness. The consummation of this process is attained in the Kingdom that is coming; we are but preparing the path for Him who comes. "Lift up your heads ye gates: let the King of Glory enter."

The application of the dynamic concept of justice evolved to the peasant calls not only for the distribution of land on an equitable basis, but also for ensuring the proper use of the same. Caught in the quagmire of eternal indebtedness, the peasant needs redress from the heavy weight of accumulated repayments that are due. He must have facilities to cultivate his land without having to mortgage fractions varying from a tenth to nine-tenths of the crop. In order that he may stay on his own two feet once he is raised, he must be enabled to develop a new attitude towards life. All these and many other vital details stem from the acceptance of a dynamic concept of justice which far exceeds the righteousness of those who find it convenient to voice demands concerning landholding for the numerous peasants.

In scaling down the indebtedness of the peasant, the process should not be allowed to encourage complacency. Probably some kind of evidence of good faith may be worked out on the basis of the average income of the peasant during the past few years, say five, and the extent of clearance that he made of his debts after the scaling down, within the next year.

Legal limits on the extent of loans that may be made to peasant will be a simultaneous necessity. Lendings beyond the limit will be at the risk of the lender, the courts refusing to enforce such loans beyond the limit. Both the lender and the borrower must be penalized in order to prevent the vicious repetition of debt, borrowing, and further debt.

The positive side of this operation of anti-debt-accumulation will naturally be arrangements for a credit supply to the peasant. One of the weakest links in this operation has been the inordinate delay in the administration of credits. "Benefit delayed is benefit denied," is a valid principle as far as the operation is concerned. Even now, by and large, the applica

tion for loans has to go through an endless hierarchy of officialdom whose interest in the welfare of the peasant is not established beyond doubt; and very often, due to the insistence on
adequate "securities," the vital loans die in the hands of the
administration. The system of securities makes it virtually impossible for any but the ablest and the most influential to get
hold of any money to tide them over the time of sowing and
manuring.

It is precisely here that the Government can help by taking
a bold step to progressively do away with the paraphernalia
of proof of ability to pay back the principal and interest. The
relative simplicity of similar operations in the United States
is something which may be advantageously applied to India.
It is inevitable that there will be some people who will try
to take advantage of the trust placed in them: the crooks are
always with us. But this has to be faced in the interests of
the nation at large. Creation of a trustworthy peasantry is an
imperative necessity for the successful running of the nation's
Development Plans. In the case of the United States, the
youthfulness of the nation, with its adventurous spirit and
bountiful resources, underwrote and continues to underwrite
the risks involved in trusting people. The rapidity with which
the finances for projects are forthcoming is matched with the
quickness with which the repayments are made in many
instances. Probably, the willingness to pay back is not a
peculiar virtue found in a prosperous situation alone. Experience of the Inter-Church-Aid to Refugees of the World Council of Churches during the last several years of its operation
shows that men and women respond to the niceties of fellow-
feeling even though they have the best reasons for a most
bitter reaction toward the whole world.

These instances urge the assumption of risks in the agricultural credit supply of the Indian peasant. There will be non-
repayment of loans in some cases: it would give headaches to
the Government to be a bill collector. But there will also be

a large number of peasants, to whom the tiny, *timely* aid, would have at once obviated the necessity for later dole. That blossoming army of honest workers, free children of full confidence, should more than compensate for the evil that some men choose to do.

It is in the building up of the impulse to respond to trust, that the participation in the political processes of power on the local level in organizations similar to the Community Coordinating Councils* in the United States can help considerably. Being trusted with money and being trusted with power are but two phases of the same facet of trust. Responsibility to run their own school or their own playground will mean much more than what the material means involved represent. For, in the Indian situation, it would mean the coming into his own of the peasant; and that is more efficacious in making him trustworthy than all the stipulations from outside can do.

Organizations similar to the Coordinating Councils can also be the agency replacing the law's delay. They can be the

---

* A Community Coordinating Council is a means through which a community discovers and meets its needs. It provides the common ground on which citizen concern, professional skill and administrative authority meet to achieve action.

"Such a council is a planning and coordinating body consisting of interested citizens, representatives of all public and private agencies, civic, religious, fraternal, business, labor, service and other groups. . . .

"Its membership includes representatives from civic, religious, service, fraternal and other groups, representatives from public and private agencies, individual citizens who may not officially represent any group but whose interests and abilities make them valuable additions to the Council. The Council is the total community in action.

"A Community Coordinating Council operates like a "Town Meeting." Problem centered committees provide an opportunity for community-wide cooperation and action. Everybody participates and decisions are made democratically.

"A delegate first talks over problems in the group to which he belongs and takes recommendations to the Council. The Council then takes action, and each delegate reports this back to his group. Member-organizations are not necessarily bound by decisions of the Council."

(Community Coordinating Councils, Los Angeles)

agencies which would vouchsafe the credit-worthiness of the needy peasant. In fact, the administration of loans through local *nonofficial* bodies will bring to bear a considerably larger pressure upon contemplating defaulters than all the nebulous distance of officialdom can. It is safe to say that the local councils will aid in the building up of what we may call *trust impulse* in the farmer, thanks to the tremendous weight of local opinion and ostracization. These councils could also be effective in ensuring that the peasants who receive aid in scaling down debts are also responsible for paying back their own dues to others.

So much for the lessening of inabilities involved in inept handling of land distribution on the negative side. The drive for lessening of inabilities must be a two-pronged thrust, both on the negative and positive sides. A brief consideration of two major means to this end on the positive side may be made here.

Owing to the recurrent needs for finance, the farmer often pledges his crop even at the time of sowing. Money lenders with little concern for the ethics of the matter get the better by inducing the farmer to sell the rest of the crop, over and above what is needed to pay for the loans, to themselves, usually at a lower price than that obtainable in the market. When the problem of credit supply is more adequately met by the agency of the councils, the peasant is freer to earn what his own crop can bring him. The council can constitute a sales agency which would handle the crop of the whole community on a co-operative basis. This experiment, so clearly successful in Switzerland, has been for so long unsuccessful in India. One of the important reasons for the failure appears to be the dichotomy in the handling of economic and political power. In Switzerland, the local levels wield quite a lot of power in moulding decisions in the nation's life; therefore, co-operative purchasing and selling agencies are but an extension of the political power they wield.

Birth control measures are indispensable if justice is to be maintained after obtaining land-holdings. The large number of children makes the fragmentation of land inevitable, the customs of inheritance being what they are. Even if land were to be justly divided among the present generation, it will soon be unjustly distributed among a flourishing family of six or seven. Therefore birth control becomes indispensable for the interests of distributive justice.

Being a novelty, birth control measures would need the concept of "sinning in good company" to make it fashionable; and here again, the councils can do a fine job. Their discussion rooms can bring sex out of the clandestine closets of popular thinking and into the open. They could confer on the merits and demerits of the different alternatives, and can facilitate the practice of some of those measures.

Discussion of these matters in the women's groups would provide an appropriate topic of interest to start them off. The fight against false modesty of the Victorian Era will be a slow one; but the number of girls passing through colleges might be a help. Anyway, in a matter involving both the sexes, enlightened co-operation of both of them is essential.

How are the peasant's abilities going to be improved? Reorganization of agricultural holdings and newer methods of cultivation are obvious necessities. Reorganization of land-holdings will require consolidation of land-holdings. In order to obtain the necessary consent of the peasants involved, pressure of opinion as well as sanction of legislation will be necessary. Pressure from the people can best be obtained on the local council level; and legislation can be made from the top, facilitating consolidation.

The co-operative nature and the corporate aspect of agricultural reorganization cannot be over-emphasized. Be it the consolidation of land or the introduction of machinery, it is a novelty; and a novelty is immediately suspect. This suspicion, and its possible evolution into opposition, can be prevented only on the council level.

The reduction of potentials arising from indebtedness, as well as the increase of abilities by better production processes, will be the prerequisites of considering distributive justice in the returns from the land to the owner, the occupant, and to the worker.

Subsistence holding is a concept used in connection with distributive justice in land returns. That holding which is able to support the farmer is roughly taken as the subsistence holding. The main principle underlying this choice is that the laborer is worthy of his reward. Based on this measure, the returns from the land are admittedly far from adequate. If the peasant were to stop and consider whether or not he should go into farming, the returns will not be something which will draw him to his work. But if he is sticking to a little plot of land out of loyalty to tradition or to ancestors, it must be remembered that the influence of these factors, will weaken with the passing of time and the change in the structural pattern of society. Economic factors are playing an increasing role in the perpetuation of traditions; migrations to towns are certainly one of the visible results of this changed attitude in the peasant. If adequate safeguards are not established, it is not unlikely that the whole system of production based on the caste divisions in Hindu society will fall into pieces. Hence appropriate returns to those laboring on the land must be assured, lest the farming population throw up their hands and walk into the nearby towns even in the face of increased population problems and absence of any promise of employment.

What should be the returns from the land? The figures naturally will vary with the place and the land. But there will be wide agreement that the returns from the land should pay off for the efforts. It should also provide a little extra to keep the incentive to cultivate. Now, this is not obtained from most of the lands under the plough today. When agricultural machinery is used widely on the farm, the returns may become more adequate to keep alive the initiative to farm. This will mean that under the present circumstances, the land returns are inadequate to be reasonably remunerative, and will remain so for a few years to come. What is to be done in the interim period in the interests of justice?

If the lands are not able to provide enough returns, and if the adequate returns are to be provided, there is immediately the question of who supplies the deficit?

In order to meet this deficit, the peasant could be bled white. He would have to go without adequate returns as he has thus far. But his motive will have to be differently oriented. While it was helplessness that made him resign himself to privation so far, now it would be a disciplined effort in the interests of the nation, similar to what he would willingly undergo in times of war, that would urge him to forego his just dues.

If bleeding the peasant white is inapplicable, taxation might be proposed as an alternative. Additional taxation for purposes of supplementing the low returns from the land will necessarily be directed upon the richer land. Roughly, it is a "Rob Peter to pay Paul" policy. However, it might not be entirely out of order as a purely interim measure. The canon of taxability will have to be applied with discernment. There will have to be consideration of the current and future productive abilities; and such a taxation will hold water only if there is reason to believe that such an effort will lead to a higher level of productivity within the period under consideration. An additional consideration in the case of land taxation is the relatively inflexible nature of agricultural operations.

Probably a more easily manageable situation is found in the field of rent. The Ricardian concept of rent hinged on the original, indestructible powers of the soil. His theory of rent depended on the differential advantage that the soil of one lot has over others. More fertile lands will naturally be cultivated first, and the enjoyment of the privilege of operating on these lands requires payment for the differential advantage. The differential advantage is measured by the no-rent margin: namely, that margin which commands no differential advantage and therefore no rent. From the differential advantage point, economic opinion shifted emphasis to returns for production, and later, to a "pure, unnecessary surplus" point of view. Land, being a factor of production, contributed to the total production and is therefore entitled to proportionate returns. Rent may be considered as the amount paid for keeping the land factor of production in operation. Pursuing this line of thought further, there is the school of thought which says that unlike the laborer, even if nothing is paid, land cannot refuse to produce; therefore, all that is paid for the use of the land is "pure, unnecessary surplus."

In a feudalistic economy such as that of India, it is a self-evident proposition that land rent must be paid for the use of land. All land belonged at one time or another to the King; and it is only good manners that there should be compensation for the use of someone else's property. Rent was therefore considered *not* as a "purely unnecessary surplus" as some theoreticians would suggest, but as a natural token of the acknowledgment of the position as a vassal. When India was brought together into more or less one piece under the British rule, they found that it was a paying proposition to take advantage of this vassal attitude. They rented the land to those who promised the highest annual revenue from the land. These bidders had only one consideration: to make money in the collection and payment of revenues to the Government.

This was probably one of the origins of the infamous "Rack-Renting" which does not recognize any canon of renting except the dictates of the situation. Exorbitant rates are charged and collected under the pain of legal enforcement. As in the case of efforts to curtail racketeering rents in populous cities, there should be both powerful legislation and vigorous enforcement of anti-rack-renting practices.

In the fight against the Communist promises of more land and more returns through revolutionary means, there is one feature that is particularly gratifying. With all his nascent unrest, the peasant is patient; and if he is convinced that something is being done for him, he is prepared to wait. He will be infuriated when the idols he visualized in the agencies of rural reconstruction fail him utterly. It is then that he becomes prepared to clutch at any odd straw that has a flag on the top of it. The two uprisings mentioned in Chapter Eleven are symptomatic of this violent betrayal that the peasant feels has been made of his confidence in organized forms of democracy. When a down-to-earth leader comes along, and pleads for his case and fights for it, the dying embers of the Indian peasant's hopes are awakened. That is one great service that Acharya Vinoba Bhave has done through his tour of the country on the Land-Gift mission. Will this opportunity be seized to quicken the hopes and sustain them in the better nature of mankind in general and Indian peasantry in particular through active efforts towards obtaining distributive justice in land-holdings as well as land returns?

CHAPTER THIRTEEN

"ONE MAN, ONE VALUE"

The laborer is worthy of his wages—the executive is also worthy of his wages—Communitarian movement—the context in which responsibility is assumed.

THE INDIAN CONSTITUTION does not prescribe any specific method for achievement of the goal of a democracy which is both economic and political: "one man, one value." What it does direct, however, is that every government, whether at the Center or in the States, should strive to bring about a democratic economic structure. In the wake of industrialization, when inanimate energy is used to multiply the efforts of human endeavor, it is necessary to examine the implications of "one man, one value" for the Indian socio-economic structure in its progressive transition from a predominantly agricultural to a predominantly industrial emphasis. Industrial returns —wages and profits—should conform to acceptable standards of distributive justice; and a just distribution should also imply certain responsibilities that go with it.

Life in the crowded streets of Calcutta adjusted itself to give way to the mile-long procession of men bearing placards and shouting slogans. They were walking three in a row. The main theme of the slogans was: *"Inquilab Zindabad,"*—Victory to Revolution. Proceeding through the main streets of the city, they were heading towards the central park where they would hold their meeting. The exploitation by the capitalists in whose factories most of the men worked would be the recurrent topic. It was almost a weekly feature.

These Saturday afternoon processions were part of the discipline that the workers found themselves subjected to in return for affiliation with a party which promised to concern itself with winning labor its rights. Irrespective of the merits or faults of the Communist alternative to *status quo,* the very fact of the industrial workers' membership in communist-sponsored organizations indicates the acute awareness of the problems of distributive justice among industrial labor.

The industrial worker is a new species in India. Regular remuneration in cash instead of irregular returns in produce, life in the city, a certain sense of pride arising out of the ability to manipulate machines—these are some of the attractions that contribute to the change of many from agriculture to industry. However, the habits that go to make an industrial worker are far from developed. Punctuality, accuracy and other essentials are not only undeveloped, but the workers are not even trained along these lines in most of the industries. Admittedly, the acquisition of such skills as are required would not be done overnight; but it is also true that such skills do not descend upon the agriculturist when he moves into town or into an industry.

One reason for the present inadequate process aimed at systematizing the acquisition of industrial skills seems to be the emphasis on distribution mentioned above. By letting production take a secondary place in relation to distribution, serious defects may originate. Two basic defects would stem from this procedure: if demands for distribution are running ahead of the supplies of production, higher returns are asked than what the production machinery is geared to achieve. It is something like starting an automobile in third gear instead of first. Second, and of graver import, is the danger of assuming rank without obligation; enjoying the privilege of being an industrial worker without the preparedness to shoulder the responsibilities stemming therefrom. In order to make sure that industrial labor is willing to assume the responsibilities pertaining to its status as a new species in a new era of national development, it should be assured that its returns shall always be fair. If such an assurance is aimed at, there should be an acceptable code of distributive justice which should have contemporaneous relevance.

> Man cannot be understood merely from the standpoint of his involvement in nature, on the one hand; nor can he, on the other, be regarded as a potentially discarnate spirit in whom historical development is progressively actualizing this potential. On the contrary, the evils to which human history is subject to arise precisely from those forms of inordinacy of natural unlimitedness of human desires and ambitions which are rooted in man's vain effort to deny his creatureliness. [1]

This attempt to deny man's creatureliness gives a new perspective to the problems of industrial returns. For one thing, this knocks the bottom out of the idolization of any humanitarian wage-fixing: the best that can be done is yet not the highest.

As the laborer is worthy of his reward, so the one who contributes his services in time, talent, and/or money is also worthy of his salt. In the early days of economic discussion about two centuries back, profit was looked upon as a reward for ownership of capital. This view was challenged by those who said that this ownership was similar to a highway post, the accident of whose location lent advantage just like a robber baron's observation post on the top of a hill. In the 18th and part of the 19th centuries, there was substantial identification between normal profit and interest.

As time went by, it was recognized on all sides that profits contain an element other than interest on capital. Distinction was made between remuneration for work and the reward for supervising business. The assumption of risk, "reward for risks not insurable," such as the failure of the whole concern and reward for the extra-productivity due to sleepless nights were some of the other reasons for profit.

Today economic theories by and large agree that profit is bound up with economic change and that it is the result of risk. With the exception of Marxists who claim the whole product for labor, most economists would agree that the profit, as part of the product of the industry, is a joint product. Differences arise in regard to splitting up this joint product.

The Employers' Association, Calcutta, India, is probably one of the very few agencies in India which has done any compilation of figures to examine the basis of present taxation in reference to distributions that can be made to different factors of production. It would be unfair, in the absence of other figures, to present these figures, which are avowedly arranged to make a plea for the private sector.

Any suggestions of profit sharing will be countered with the reply that that would be almost the last straw which would break the industrial camel's back. According to the Association, most of the industries are on the lowest level of subsistence, some of them living on the past accumulation of profits which are fast being depleted. Depreciation allowances are not anywhere near adequate; even if the present rate of depreciation were to be doubled, it would still leave most of the industries with no undistributed profits, and some with negative balances.

New industries are needed and old ones have to be renovated. What considerations shall govern the allocation of resources? Be it new industries or renovations of the old, capital wants early profits; and simultaneously labor, a share of the big money. In this context, should profits be undistributed or shared? It is a question which has to be answered on the merit of individual situations as they arise. However, two broad principles may be generally borne in mind in dealing with profits.

One is that the profit-motive as such is not to be condemned. The Commission on "The Responsible Society in a World Perspective" of the World Council of Churches wrote in its final report:

> The churches have been properly critical of monopolistic practices, and of the effects of many irresponsible business practices on people and society generally. But they also need to understand and lay stress on the valuable contribution which the skilled executive has to make to society, irrespective of the form of ownership or organization. At its best, the business system has provided incentives for the responsible initiative and hard work which produces economic progress, and has embodied the wisdom of decentralized decisions and widely distributed power. These are virtues needed in any system. [2]

The second principle to be recognized is that the laborer who asks for profit sharing is really asking for a share in the control of industry. Profits are merely one form of accumulation of the results of a joint endeavor, and the suggestion for profit sharing is really the suggestion for sharing in the good fruits of the industry as a whole.

In this demand, it would appear that privileges are preceding responsibilities, and profits production. But it is neither advisable, nor perhaps feasible, to hold off the day of profit sharing. If one wants to learn how to swim, it is imperative that he must be prepared for the first few gulps of water. In the long run, there may be little escape from the fact of the sharing of both production and profits between capital and labor. He will be wise who reads the writing on the wall and prepares for a peaceful adjustment. Rights, when pressed for as denied demands, can assume quite a sharp edge.

Even in granting these rights of sharing, there can be a vitiating impersonality which can completely ruin the wisdom in the preparedness for change. Here again we come across the central problem of treating human beings as brothers because of the Fatherhood of God. The laborer who pleads for profit sharing, for power, is really asking for his right to be treated as a brother in the family of mankind. No crumbs from the table of the rich would satisfy him; he would rather look for the poorest fare in the firm where he is accepted as he is, in his rights, not as the human form of a modern gadget. Only this sense of belonging can solve the basic problems of profit sharing.

This is not making the problem any easier. But there is no shortcut to human understanding; the first step is to enter into it as a problem in human relationships. And proper entry calls for the prerequisite of a definite view about the basis of human relationship, which, to repeat, is not an occasional feeling of big brotherliness, but something in obedience to the Divine Imperative: Thou shalt love thy neighbor as thyself.

Many will not understand this: both among capital and labor. The former might find this approach smacking of cowardice; the latter might be suspicious of something so wonderful. It is here that excellent service can be done by men with a vision, who in their lives enjoy the assurance that while there is no straight line from human labors to the Kingdom of God, in the Lord, their labor is not thrown away.

There are around one hundred Communities of Work in Europe, mainly in France, but also some in Belgium, Switzerland and Holland. Some of them are industrial, and some of them are agricultural. They differ among themselves in various aspects; nevertheless the basic principles are sufficiently similar. . . .

Boimondau is a watch-case factory. In fact, it has become one of the seven largest such factories in France. It was founded by Marcel Barbu. . . . After the French defeat in 1940, Barbu wanted to have a factory of his own, where he introduced a factory council and a wage approved by all, including sharing in the profits . . . He went out into the streets, and found a barber, a sausage-maker, a waiter—practically anyone except specialized industrial workers. The men were all under thirty. He offered to teach them watch-case making, provided they would agree to *search* with him for a setup in which the "distinction between employer and employee would be abolished" . . . as they were not out just for a better economic setup but a new way of living together, discussions were bound to lead to the disclosure of basic attitudes. "Very soon" says Barbu, "we saw the necessity of a common basis, or what we called, from then on, our common ethics. . . ."

The second discovery the group made was that they craved to educate themselves. They figured out that the time they saved on production could be used for education. Within three months, the productivity of their work grew so much, that they could save nine hours on a forty-eight-hour week. What did they do? They used these nine hours for education and were paid for it as for regular work hours. First they wanted to sing well together, then to polish their French grammar, then to learn how to read business accounts. From there, other courses developed, all given at the factory by the best instructors they could find. The instructors were paid the regular rates. There were courses in engineering, physics, literature, Marxism, Christianity, dancing, singing and basket ball.

Their principle is: "We do not start from the plant, from the technical activity of man, but from man himself . . . In a Community of Work accent is not on *acquiring* together, but on *working together* for a collective and personal fulfillment." The aim is not increased productivity, or higher wages, but a new style of life which "far from relinquishing the advantages of the industrial revolution, is adapted to them. . . ."

From a civilization of objects to a civilization of persons: better even—a civilization of movement between persons. [3]

The Communitarian Movement which Fromm describes as "this penetrating and thoughtful work, one of the most enlightening ones dealing with the psychological problems of industrial organization and the possibilities for the future" is definitely worth considering in the Indian context.

Harmony in communication depends on the power of transmission as well as that of reception. If the transmitting unit is too large for the receiving set, there is bound to be waste; if the transmitting unit is too small for the receiving set, there is bound to be inadequacy. Imbalance might result in apoplexy at the transmission end and anemia at the reception end. "Water, water everywhere, but not a drop to drink." Power, power everywhere, but not a whit to move anything. In the case of an automobile, this situation is analogous to the "racing" of the motor. The motor of national emancipation produces considerable power; but the gear is in neutral position. Result: the wheels of production do not move, even when the exultant sense of national emancipation goes on roaring.

But when the gear is shifted to low, the mechanism begins to come to life. Maybe the next shifts can be made quickly: the motor might already be producing enough power to permit shifting to high gear. In either case, the start having been in neutral, a time-lag has to be allowed. The lag between enjoyment of privileges and shouldering of responsibility might be compared to the lag between seeing the lightning and hearing the thunder. This is portentious.

This portentious lag arises out of at least two kinds of adjustment. They relate to inter-power and intrapower unitary transmission. Inter-transmission may be used to refer to transmission between the nation and the smaller component units, i.e., communities, families, etc. Intra-transmission would connote the process of appropriation of the sense of possession so obtained by the constituent members of the family.

That the most dominant note in the speeches of the Indian leaders after the attainment of Independence has been the behest to assume responsibilities, is no accident. They were urging the channeling of inter-transmission. Units of local government in villages are a step in this direction: to make the different units of people appropriate what the nation won for them. In industrial situations, the trade unions play the role of constituting the receiving end of the industrial community for inter-transmission.

The success or otherwise of inter-transmission depends on intra-transmission. One recalls the vivid faces of the peasants in the village, who, pointing to the Indian Flag, queried where food was. Here the intra-transmission was showing its weak spots. The sense of newly acquired power was not accompanied by a corresponding sense of responsibility: they ought to have asked the question and answered it themselves, because, even as they acquired the freedom to ask for food, they also had been invested with the responsibility to find food.

It is in this context of the excited hopes, understandably exaggerated, of the people as individuals and family units concerning the potentialities and the promise of the new national power and the inadequacies of their personal realization, that industrial strikes are paraded as fights for justice. Whenever there are problems of power involved, distributive justice has an alluring, almost irresistible appeal.

No one can deny the role of fights for justice, particularly in the context of *de novo* establishment of standards of conduct. However, the soundness of the fights for justice will have to derive justification from their role in making effective the inter- and intra-transmissions. The raising of wages or lowering of working hours are no ends in themselves. They are significant only to the extent that they enable the people to appropriate their share of national pride along with their share of national responsibility. More money without a proper perspective of the use of it will defeat the very purpose of the fights for justice. If it is only higher wages that are secured, it is a sad sacrifice of, and poor payment for, the new sense of personal emancipation, consequent on the new sense of national emancipation.

Thus there are the elements of justice and power pulling themselves apart. Justice and power cannot be resolved outside love. When the child asks for pampering and the parents refuse outright, the justice in their action keeps the child from estrangement only in the love that binds the family. If the love governing their relationship is not forceful enough to enable the family to outlive the operation of justice, estrangement results. Continuous scolding, repeated spanking, and other home-patented means of correction would be dreadful in their execution of justice if love did not take the edge off them.

On a national level, when we ask for responsibility, we are asking for a parallel relationship. The trade unions which demand justice must also realize the vital role of labor in the production machinery of the nation. This recognition can come only from love for the nation. In its context, privileges are asserted and simultaneously sustained by shouldered responsibilities.

Practising love in national life is far more exacting than practising justice: the former, the divine imperative, is far more demanding than the latter, which is a human institution to approximate the former.

PART IV

Contours of Construction

CHAPTER FOURTEEN

CLOUDS OF THE SIZE OF
A MAN'S HAND

AT THE END OF THREE YEARS and six months during which there was neither dew nor rain, Elijah the prophet prayed for rain in Israel.

> And Elijah went up to the top of Carmel; and he cast himself down upon the earth, and put his face between his knees,
> And said to his servant, Go up now, look toward the sea. And he went up, and looked, and said, There is nothing. And he said, Go again seven times.
> And it came to pass at the seventh time, that he said, Behold, there ariseth a little cloud out of the sea, like a man's hand. And he said, Go up, say unto Ahab, Prepare thy chariot, and get thee down, that the rains stop thee not. [1]

The contours of construction are like clouds of the size of a man's hand. Even as the clouds so small are almost insignificant against the vast expanse of the sky, so are the contours light in comparison with the rising expanse of portents. Yet India is involved in a battle to see if she or any other country trusting in the principles of human dignity will survive. And, similar to the wavering flicker of candlelight conquering encircling darkness, these small promises will conquer the portents.

The strain on human endurance is increased considerably

when the prospect of better living is dangled before a people who have nothing to lose except their sense of values and cherished traditions. Whether ends should justify the means or the means the end, can not for long be continued as an agonizing appraisal.

It will be easier to take stock of the situation if the main elements are identified. One of the lectures delivered at the Annual Institute held in Chicago under the auspices of the Norman Wait Harris Memorial Foundation took stock of the situation from the point of view of the West:

> For the time being the challenge which confronts the West in its efforts to deny the underdeveloped areas of Southeast Asia to the Communist appeal is therefore compounded of two distinct elements. The more obvious of these is, of course, the problem of depriving the Communists of their actual and potential "mass base" by an adequate program of technical aid and economic reform designed to *remove the blight of poverty* from the scheme of things heretofore in force in these areas. The other and more imponderable aspect of this two-fold challenge requires the *development of an ethos and system of values* which can compete successfully with the attraction exercised by communism *for* those sections of the *native intelligentsia* which have been the source and mainstay of its leadership. To date, there is little evidence that the West is prepared to meet either of these challenges on terms commensurate with their gravity. [2] (italics supplied)

One qualification to this anlysis as applied to India would be that the removal of the blight of poverty should be via programs that are germane to the mores and customs of the people and in a manner that is fulfilling the destiny of the people more efficiently; and that the common man asks for a faith that can command his full commitment even as the intellectual. Remember Chester Bowles's Fundamental questions:

Last but not least what about India's greatest natural resources—her young people? Today many thousands of students in India are frustrated and insecure. How rapidly and
fully can these potentially explosive intellectuals be tied
into the dynamic growth of India? [3]

The "explosive intellectuals" are not nursing their frustration and biding their time.

Enough empirical material exists to warrant the conclusion
that the "colonial" Communist parties of Asia today, as in the
1920's, are the handiwork of native intellectuals. Since 1940,
they have, of course, greatly expanded their mass following
and membership, but their leadership is still drawn overwhelmingly from the intellegentsia . . . India illustrates the
same trend. Its earliest Communist leadership is exemplified
in M. N. Roy (who later broke with the movement), a high-
caste Brahmin of considerable intellectual attainments. Also
indicative of the predominance of intellectuals in the leadership of the Indian Communist party is the fact that, at its
first All-India Congress in 1943, 86 of a total attendance of
139 delegates were members of professional and intellectual
groups. . . . [4]

This tide waits for no man and for no nation. It has to be met
head-on with resoluteness and humility, with a perspective
wide enough to be true to India's greatness and with a philosophy of action built on faith and family. National in compass,
the concerted effort should inspire every remote peasant; for
it is his soul that is being fought for, his family that is being
defended, his freedom that is being won.

The contours are somewhat small—in the form of the illit-
erate peasants' hopes for betterment of their lot; in the struggles of a few young men; in the inspiration of a handful of
leaders.

Will India go Communist?

CHAPTER FIFTEEN

CONCRETE PROJECTS FOR
CONTEMPORARY TIMES

An objective assessment service in India—suggested organizational features—possible sponsorship—simultaneous projects: worship place; birth control clinic; rural industrial center; educational body—Will India go Communist?

FRUSTRATED IDEALISM, dammed energy—the Devil and Communism have use for them. Frustration can be avoided only by fulfillment. In order to provide for fulfillment, the potentials are to be assessed carefully, and appropriate channels of expression are to be made available to the young Indian. The need for such assessment has long since been recognized and recorded by a succession of Commissions on University Education, the latest being the commission appointed by the Government of India in December, 1948.

This Commission imperatively urged the introduction of objective tests ("Test" and "examination" are used as interchangeable.) for admission, achievement, evaluation and guidance purposes. This section outlines a plan to execute the Commission's recommendation.

The Commission stressed the inefficiency of the existing system of examinations in evaluating student progress. It also noted the great need for vocational guidance and the necessity for providing scholarship aids to the many able students who cannot afford higher education. These remarks assume fresh significance when it is recalled that the numerical membership of the age group 15–25 in India is around 68.5 million[1] as against the corresponding figure of 22.0 million[2] in the United States. The potential college population of India is thus more than three times that of the United States. But, of the 68.5 million potential, only about 0.3 million[3] ever get to institutions of higher education. Against this 0.4 per cent in India, enrollment in U.S. higher educational institutions of 2.5 milliion in the fall of 1954[4] represented 11.3 per cent.

Thus the introduction of objective tests is aimed at rectifying two major defects of the Indian educational system: (1), more efficient equipment of the students who go to institutions of higher learning by a new emphasis on the use of mental faculties required by objective tests and, (2), more efficient channeling of potential students according to the aptitudes and abilities that are evidenced. Admittedly, the first objective will be easier to accomplish than the second, both from a technical and practical standpoint.

Assessment of achievement is called for not only at the final examinations of the universities which grant diplomas on the basis of performance in these examinations, but also by the Public Service Commissions. In a land where a heavy premium is attached to government jobs, the prestige of these examinations definitely rates very highly. And since the examination system and the examination procedures are similar, the Commission's observations on the subject are pertinent to both the university and the Public Service Commission examinations.

> For nearly half a century, examinations, as they have been functioning, have been recognized as one of the worst features of Indian education ... The obvious deficiencies and harmful consequences of this most pervasive evil in Indian education have been analysed and set out clearly by successive Universities Commissions since 1902, by a Government Resolution as far back as 1904 and by a Committee of the

Central Advisory Board of Education in recent years. With most of their criticism we are in agreement and do not wish to dilate on the patent defects and dangers of this system. We only note that *while the magnitude of the problem has been growing* at an alarming rate *nothing constructive in the way of reform has happened.* . . .

A university degree is a kind of passport for jobs. With the great economic pressure due to the prevailing poverty in the country, the insistence on a university degree as the minimum requirement even for posts of minor officials and clerks puts a *premium on a number of evils* which have come to be *associated with the examination system* . . . The obsession to secure, as it were, a ticket in the lottery of job-securing has overshadowed the educational purposes which a good examination can serve. . . .

We are convinced that if we are to suggest *one single reform* in the university education it *should be that of the examinations.* . . .[5] (Italics supplied)

"This most pervasive evil" that the Commission refers to, applies equally well to the Public Service Commission examinations as it does to the University examinations. The practice of "cramming" which has sprung up in the wake of these examinations is a scandalous comment on the method of the examination. Cramming is the order of the day and the premium on independent thinking is extremely low under a system of examinations which puts such weight on rote repetition of borrowed phrases.

A lamentable consequence of this type of accepted short cut to professional positions is the continuation of lopsided social values. The dignity of labor means next to nothing in India. Prestige and social standing go with the number of people who look up to you, the number of errand-runners, and the initials after your name.

The appropriate emphasis on sound methods of learning and of the necessity to use one's faculties would be the first step towards correcting the lopsidedness that is killing initiative today. The proof of the pudding is in passing the examination and not in being able to use your head. When once that stock goes down, and examinations for which you can never cram are in vogue, there would be some chance for initiative to be encouraged, able administrators to be recruited, and some separation of the wheat from the chaff. It will be a long time before matters of the mind assume superiority over matters of snobbishness, but a good beginning can be made by putting the premium on original thinking as is done in objective tests.

The Bureau of Education[6] showed that 86 per cent of the boys and 93 per cent of the girls who were in Class I in 1929-30 were not to be found in Class V in 1933-34. The situation remains pretty much the same in 1955. When the literacy in India is as low as 18 per cent, those who somehow get to the portals of institutions of learning constitute a vital source of national intellectual potential. And a majority of them are left uncared for to such an extent that they remain flowers that bloom and wither in the wilderness.

Discovery of human talents such as is represented in the drop-out majority can be attempted through the use of objective tests of aptitude.* However, as mentioned earlier, this is a long-term goal. The immediate attention may be turned to influencing the current examination system, because the examination is the gateway to the means of livelihood in India. This narrow pathway is treacherous and needs immediate rectification.

Thus, the immediate objectives of an Objective Testing Organization in India are the development, administration, analysis and interpretation of objective tests for admission,

---

* *Aptitude*: A condition or set of characteristics regarded as symptomatic of an individual's ability to acquire with training some (usually specified) knowledge, skill or set of responses, such as ability to speak a language, to produce music . . .

H. C. Warren, *Dictionary of Psychology*, Boston: Houghten Mifflin, 1934.

achievement, evaluation and guidance purposes, or, briefly, aptitude and achievement tests. The development of such tests should be based on clearly stated principles, both of education and testing. The enunciation of these principles should be undertaken by a comptent body of Indian and American experts who would also keep in view the application of these principles in the development of tests which would eventually replace current examinations. The linguistic basis of redrawing the map of India indicates the necessity for tests in all the 14 regional languages as well as English. The nature and function of an organization which can efficiently serve the needs of objective testing in India will be discussed next.

The advantages of a larger unit than that of the region for objective testing may be seen in reference to the various processes in objective testing. First of all, in specifying the qualities that the universities would consider pertinent to admission, the Inter-University Board would be indicated as better endowed than the individual universities themselves. Through the Board, the smaller universities as well as the larger ones can clear their several ideas in relation to the ideal set of qualities to be tested, and agree upon one such set which will be nationally accepted. Such sets will be subject to periodic review.

Secondly, test construction is a technical job calling for experts. Admittedly, experts are more easily congregated under national auspices than regional. In the wake of linguistic division of the country, tests in 14 or 15 languages will be a desirable goal. While catering to this cultural need, care has to be exercised to leave scientific operations like test construction unhampered by cultural considerations. One way to combine both these requisites will be to construct the tests in the different languages on a nationally agreed variety of topics and difficulty levels in a central office. The proximity to experts working on similar tests can be utilized for promoting scientific accuracy by providing for reviews of tests by bilingual experts

Thirdly, test production requires utmost security. A large number of university examinations in India have been subject to "leakage" of question papers. In order to minimize such hazards, it will be advisable to produce the tests in the same place where they are constructed. Photo-offset printing can be used with advantage. Here again, the installation of machinery in one central spot will be prudent.

Fourthly, test administration may be carried out through the different universities themselves, at least for the first five years. During this period, the objective tests can be administered as an additional examination over and above the current essay-type examinations. The results of the essay and objective examinations may be studied to provide the necessary basis for developing a set of objective examinations which may progressively take the place of essay examinations.

Fifthly, test analysis would require the setting up of statistical and computational machinery. Since the process of grading standardized tests is uniform, there seems to be no reason for installing scoring and other allied machinery all over the country.

Test interpretation will remain the prerogative of the users of tests. Statistical analysis and other aids will merely be evidences presented. The final decision and action on the basis of these evidences would always rest with the users.

The foregoing description outlines a national organization for objective testing in India which will work in close cooperation with the universities and other agencies engaged in testing, or interested in selection by means of tests. In establishing such an agency on a national scale, it is essential that Indian personnel should be well-trained to handle the job. Since India does not possess adequate technical know-how, it will be advisable to seek help in the matter. In their report, the University Commission referred to the College Entrance Examination Board in the United States of America as a welcome source of guidance. When the Commission visited the United States, a larger organization extending the work of the College Board was just established under the title: Educational Testing Service (abbreviated as ETS). ETS unites in a single organization the educational testing functions formerly performed by the American Council of Education, the College Entrance Examination Board, and the Carnegie Foundation for the Advancement of Teaching. In addition to the comprehensive testing operations that it undertakes (2,000,000 tests every year), ETS, in the words of the Board of Trustees, "will hope to stimulate research and sound testing procedure everywhere and to help educators who feel a need for guidance in the selection, use, and interpretation of tests." Therefore it seems reasonable to think in terms of technical assistance through this competent testmaking body in the United States.

In the discussions already held with top-ranking ETS officers, it has been made clear that while ETS is anxious not to thrust tests on anybody, it would be glad to render all possible assistance to establishing objective testing on a national scale in India.

This assistance can be most fruitful and conducive to the development in India of not only objective testing but also a philosophy of education. In order to effectively achieve this, the benefit of constant consultation with the experts of ETS is essential. These consultations should pertain to both the day-to-day testing operations in India and to the overall philosophy governing such testing. Out of the healthy, vigorous exchange of views, India can hope to evolve something of lasting value to her educational system. The continuing cooperation during the first five or ten years could possibly take shape in the form of: (1), the training of Indian educators in the United States; (2), the services of technical consultants and field work coordinators with whom Indian educators can plan to organize efficiently the work of objective testing in India; and, (3), the rendering of evaluation and advisory service by the United States organization in respect to the research activities of the Indian objective testing organization and the training of Indian educators abroad. The special training of a few high-powered Indian testmakers by itself would be only a minor part of the technical cooperation that would be called for.

The organization appropriate to bring about this result seems to be two councils—Indian and American Councils—of the national organization for testing in India. The membership of the one council would be entirely Indian. The other council should necessarily have representatives of ETS. It would be desirable to have one Indian member to represent Indian education on the American Council. It would be probably helpful if this member were to be associated with the Ministry of Education in India.

The councils could have seven members each. The Indian Council would probably consist of one representative from each of the agencies that would be immediately involved in testing: The Ministry of Education, The Inter-University Board, The Union Public Service Commission, The State Public Service Commissions, and The Planning Commission. The executive secretary of the Indian Council could be a nominee of the Ministry of Education. So also the executive secretary of the American Council, a nominee of ETS.

The five agencies listed above appear to be the ones who will be immediately interested in objective testing. As users of tests, it will only be legitimate for them to underwrite the operating expenses of the testing operations.

The initial outlay of expenditure for buildings, machinery, etc. appear to be somewhat heavy for Indian agencies to bear alone. Indo-American Technical Cooperation Plan may be indicated as a possible source of financial sponsorship for the large non-recurring overhead expenses. The Ford and Carnegie Foundations in the United States, by virtue of their interest in education, also may conceivably be sources of support for the permanent overhead expenses.

Objective testing visualized in India is both educational and vocational (which includes professional). The connotation to Indian people will be the major consideration in choosing a name which describes succintly and correctly the intended operations. Testing by itself is an age-old institution; in fact, the universities are the agencies which conduct academic examinations. The core of the new testing operations seems to be the emphasis on objective type, as distinguished from somewhat subjective type of evaluations which creep in rather heavily in essay-type examinations. Another feature will be the "Service" nature of it. By "Service" is implied a concept not common in India. The testing service will provide the results of the tests to the users of tests; the interpretation and the use of the tests are up to the users themselves. In this respect the "Service" is a novelty. Therefore, "Objective" and "Service" seem to be two key words. The nature of operations visualized is probably well described by the word "Assessment." Thus, OBJECTIVE ASSESSMENT SERVICE seems to be a suitable title, easily abbreviated to OAS.

While on the national level, the key project would aim at discovering and directing the explosive intellectual potential, on the local level, four simultaneous projects would comprise the forging ahead in the battle for the people's personality.

The biggest bulwark against the sweeping victory of communism in India is the inner questioning in the minds of men about the context of their lives. It is this questioning that has considerably aided in stalling the assertion that dialectical determinism has all the answers. But the questioning needs some indication of an answer. Eternal truths cannot be explained by pat formulae: they have to be freshly discovered in and through personal lives. And the most effective means of promoting such personal discovery is the creation of circumstances conducive to the pursuit of these verities.

In concrete terms, more than the building of worship centers in the community, is needed the construction of *com-*

munity life around the worship center. This centrality does not call for certain rituals, but it does call for certain codes of conduct which should set the tempo of the general activity engaged in by the community as a corporate entity.

It is no accident that this centrality was discovered as basic to the entire communitarian movement as was pointed out in Chapter Thirteen.

> Unless there was a common ethical basis, there was no point to start from together and therefore no possibility of building anything. To find a common ethical basis was not easy, because the two dozen workers now engaged were all different: Catholics, Protestants, materialists, humanists, atheists, Communists. They all examined their own individual ethics, that is, of what they, out of their own experiences and thoughts, found necessary.

> They discovered that their individual ethics had certain points in common. They took those points and made them the common minimum on which they agreed unanimously. It was not a theoretical, vague declaration. In their forward they declared: "There is no danger that our common ethical minimum should be an arbitrary convention, for, in order to determine the points we rely on life experiences. All our moral principles have been tried in real life, everyday life, everybody's life. . . ."[7]

Commitment arising out of reflection is what the worship center focus of community life should aim at. Since everybody in India professes one religion or another, the worship center of the community should be one where the follower of every religion can pause to worship. Aids to worship, if used, may lead to the defeat of the very purpose of a common worship center. An appropriately large hall, simple but serene, should be an ideal choice. And that place should be used for no purpose other than that of providing the atmosphere conducive to active contemplation.

The construction of such a worship center will necessitate

substantial exchange and expression of ideals on the local level. Insistence upon maintaining indigenous architecture and indigenous decorative art-work in the construction of the worship center should send the people scurrying for original ideas. A worship place is something in which institutionalized values will stimulate universal participation. Once the construction of such a center is afoot, the people of the village would have had plenty of experience in pulling together instead of against one another.

"Why Not a Ministry of Population?" was Julian Huxley's view on the population problem in India. Setting up an entire ministry to look after the problem would be indicative of the earnest awareness of the magnitude of the problem and the keen interest in solving it. So also, the villagers must be urged to set up a ministry of population on their level. Equipment and fittings for the clinic, examination tables, instrument cabinets, sterilizers, educational materials, stationery and contingencies would constitute non-recurring expenses. Compensations paid to a part-time lady doctor, a full-time Health Visitor, and a nurse would be the main recurring expenses. It may be worthwhile to make the grants from the Government towards recurring and non-recurring expenses contingent upon the people constructing a suitable building for the purpose. Once the clinic is established, the cost per patient at the clinic may be adjusted to bring the facilities to everyone in need. In Bombay, cost per patient at the clinic where there is a special staff is reported to be 7 Rupees on account of establishment plus 6 Rupees for appliances, making a total of 13 Rupees ($2.73).[8]

Ambar Charka could probably be the nucleus of the industrial center of the village community. After popularizing the Ambar Charka, iron ploughs may be popularized through the industrial center. This direct relevance to the farmer's needs in terms of mechanical means of cultivation would serve to make the industrial center a vital spot in the rural life's transition from a predominantly agricultural to a predominantly industrial structure.

Adult education should not content itself with teaching adults merely how to read and write. The use of TV as an educational medium may be advantageously channeled to fortify the process of synthetic judgment of the numerous peasants. News, rather than views, would be indicated to be the welcome means to this end.

Portentious times with their promises weigh the question: "Will India go Communist?" Will suppressed aspirations, stifled ambitions and frustrated idealisms join forces to occasion a historic-deterministic explosion of India's ancient mores and customs? Or, will better sense prevail, and construction get the better of destruction?

The time is running out. Unsatisfied hunger, increasing numbers of mouths to be fed, and dimming prospects of betterment press for resourcefulness, resoluteness and readiness of measures to meet the situation.

Unaided, India would find it more difficult to meet the multitudinous perplexities that confront her.

Her determination to court the disadvantage of using clean means in dirty situations, her decision not to sell her soul for any mess of pottage, and her fervent hopes for the values of truth, peace and human dignity that she shares with all freedom-loving peoples, look forward to fulfillment in the context of increased international understanding.

NOTES

PART I

Chapter One

1. Fydor Dostoyevsky, *The Brothers Karamazov*, Random House, Modern Library, New York, 1950, pages 300, 302.

Chapter Two

1. J. R. Hicks, *The Theory of Wages*, Peter Smith, Gloucester, Mass., 1957, page 229.

2. Jawharlal Nehru, in a speech delivered before German Foreign Policy Association at Koenigswinter, *The New York Times*, July 16, 1956, page 3.

3. Vijaya Lakshmi Pandit, as quoted in the *Atlantic Monthly*, Supplement on India, 1953.

4. Norman Cousins, "Two Conversations in Asia," *Saturday Review of Literature*, December, 1953.

5. Arnold Toynbee, *The World and the West*, Oxford, London, 1953.

6. Reinhold Niebhur, "Christianity and the Moral Law," *Christian Century*, December, 1953.

7. Chester Bowles, *Ambassador's Report*, Harper, New York, 1954, page 200.

8. *Letter to the Presbyterian Churches*, Office of the General Assembly, Philadelphia, October 21, 1953, page 5.

PART II

Chapter Four

1. United Nations, *Preliminary Report on World Social Conditions*, New York, United Nations Economic and Social Council, April, 1952, page 1 (mimeographed edition).

2. United Nations, Food Agriculture Organization, *The State of Food and Agriculture*, New York, 1952.

3. *Indiagram* No. 781, January, 1956, issued by the Indian Embassy, Washington, D. C.

4. Jacob Viner, "The Role of the United States in the World Economy," in Robert Lekachman ed., *National Policy for Economic Welfare at Home and Abroad*, Doubleday, New York, 1955, page 231.

5. Satya Swaroop, *Probable Effect of Decrease in Infantile Mortality on Future Population*, Census of India, Paper No. 3, 1949, pages 1, 2.

6. Ruth Young, "Some Aspects of Birthcontrol in India," *Marriage Hygiene*, First series, Volume 2, (August, 1935), page 39.

7. *Holy Bible*, King James Version, Genesis 38:9.

8. *The New York Times*, September 10, 1954.

9. V. M. Dandekar and Kumudini Dandekar, *Survey of Fertility and Mortality in Poona District*, Poona, 1954.

10. C. Chandrasekaran, "Opinion Research in Human Fertility," in *Report of the Proceedings, Second All India Conference on Family Planning*, The Central Office, Family Planning Association of India, Bombay, page 45.

11. A. E. Hotchner, "Global TV is on the Way," *Reader's Digest*, May, 1955, page 64.

12. Kingsley Davis and Judith Blake, "Social Structure and Fertility: An Analytic Framework," *Economic Development and Cultural Change*, University of Chicago, Vol. IV, No. 3, April 1956.

13. Family Planning Research and Programs Committee, New Delhi, 1955.

14. *Ibid.*

15. P. K. Whelpton, "Too Many People in the World?", *U. S. News & World Report*, July 13, 1956, page 90.

16. Harvey Libenstein, *A Theory of Economic-Demographic Development*, Princeton University Press, Princeton, 1954.

Chapter Five

1. *Census of India*, 1951, Manager of Publications, Delhi, 1953, Vol. I, Part I-A, page 40.

2. Charles Dickens, *A Tale of Two Cities*, Random House, New York, 1950, page 98.

3. *The New York Times*, January 23, 1956, Financial Section, page 32.

Chapter Six

1. W. Somerset Maugham, "The Kite," in *Quartet,* Doubleday, New York, 1949, page 121.
2. Somerset Maugham, *op. cit.,* page 122.
3. Erich Fromm, *"The Sane Society,"* Reinhart, New York, 1955, page 45.
4. Erich Fromm, *op. cit.,* pages 52, 53.
5. Adlai E. Stevenson, 1954, Godkin Lectures at Harvard University, Harvard, Massachusetts.
6. Chester Bowles, "Some Fundamental Questions," in *Kurukshetra,* monthly organ of the Community Development Projects Administration, Publications Division, Delhi, May, 1955, page 13.

Chapter Eight

1. Arnold Toynbee, *The World and the West,* Oxford, London, 1953.
2. Margaret Mitchell, *Gone With the Wind,* Doubleday, New York, 1954, pages 130, 616.
3. *Holy Bible,* Authorized Version, Daniel 4:30. "The king spake, and said, Is not this great Babylon, that I have built for the house of the kingdom by the might of my power, and for the honor of my majesty?"
4. Will Herberg, *Protestant, Catholic, Jew,* Doubleday, New York, 1956, pages 88, 89, 92.
5. *The New York Times,* August 18, 1956, page 9.
6. Will Herberg, *op. cit.,* pages 286, 287.

Chapter Nine

1. C. G. Jung, "The Love Problem of the Student," in John Francis McDermott ed., *The Sex Problem In Modern Society,* Random House, New York, 1931, pages 346, 347.
2. C. G. Jung, *op. cit.,* page 346.
3. Arthur Hugh Clough, "With Whom There is No Variableness," as quoted in D. T. Niles, *The Word of God,* Christian Literature Society, Ceylon, 1945, page 8.
4. World Council of Churches, *Report of the Advisory Commission on the Main Theme,* 1954, paragraph 25.
5. World Council of Churches, *op. cit.,* paragraph 6.
6. Rabindra Nath Tagore, *Gitanjali,* MacMillan, London, 1914, pages 27, 28.

Chapter Ten

1. *Indian Express* (English Daily newspaper), Madras, April 22, 1954.

2. *Kurukshetra*, monthly organ of the Community Projects Administration, Publications Division, Delhi, April, 1955, page 33.

3. *Loc. cit.*

4. Robert C. Kingsbury, "India's Industrial Growth," *Focus*, The American Geographical Society, New York, Vol. VI, No. 9, May, 1956.

5. A. M. Rosenthal, "India Faces Crucial Year; Needs Aid to Meet Goals," *The New York Times*, January 4, 1956, page 84.

6. *Holy Bible*, Authorized Version, James 2:15,16.

7. John Von Neumann and Oskar Morgenstern, *The Theory of Games and Economic Behavior*, Princeton University Press, Princeton, 1947.

8. Neumann and Morgenstern, *op. cit.*, page 8.

9. For further clarification see George K. Chacko, "Certain Game Situations in Regional Economic Development," *Indian Journal of Economics*, October, 1956.

10. Dudley Ward ed., *Goals of Economic Life*, Harper, New York, 1953, pages 15, 16.

11. A. M. Rosenthal, "Asian Lands Shun Unity on U.S. Aid," *The New York Times*, May 13, 1955.

12. Translated from the German by T. W. Hutchinson, *The Significance and Basic Postulates of Economic Theory*, MacMillan, 1938, page 165.

PART III

Chapter Twelve

1. Ward, *op. cit.*, pages 441, 442.

Chapter Thirteen

1. Ward, *op. cit.*, page 445.

2. World Council of Churches, Evanston, 1954, Document 103-AC, paragraph 21:3.

3. Claire Huchet Bishop, *All Things Common*, Harper, New York, 1950, as quoted in Erich Fromm, *The Sane Society*, Reinhart, New York, 1955, pages 306-310.

PART IV

Chapter Fourteen

1. *Holy Bible,* Authorized Version, 1 Kings, 18:42, 43, 44.

2. Morris Watnick, "The Appeal of Communism to the Under-developed Peoples," in Bert F. Hoselitz ed., *The Progress of Under-developed Areas,* Chicago University Press, Chicago, 1952, page 172.

3. Chester Bowles, "Some Fundamental Questions," in *Kurukshetra,* Monthly Organ of the Community Projects Administration, Publications Division, Delhi, May, 1955, page 13.

4. Watnick, *op. cit.,* pages 162, 163.

Chapter Fifteen

1. Kingsley Davis, *The Population of India and Pakistan,* Princeton University Press, Princeton, 1951, page 157. (used as a basis for projection)

2. U.S. Bureau of the Census.

3. *The Report of the University Education Commission,* Vol. I, Manager of Publications, Delhi, 1950, page 346. (used as a basis for projection)

4. U.S. Office of Education, as quoted in *The World Almanac,* 1956, page 481.

5. *The Report of the University Commission, op. cit.,* pages 327, 329.

6. *Education in India in 1933–34,* Manager of Publications, Delhi, 1936, pages 40, 56, as quoted in Kingsley Davis, *op. cit.,* page 160.

7. Erich Fromm, *The Sane Society,* Rinehart, New York, 1955, pages 333, 334.

8. V. V. Puri, "Family Planning in the Municipal Health Services," *Report of the Proceedings, Second All-India Conference on Family Planning,* Bombay, 1955, page 91.

INDEX